"I'm very grateful for this new book, *Executive Influence*, which spotlights men and women of character and conviction in today's workplace. I am especially grateful to see the spotlight on my good friend David Weekley who has partnered with us to care for his employees and their family members."

Gil A. Stricklin, founder and president,
Marketplace Ministries, Inc.

"There are many views as to how a Christian can have a positive impact for Christ in the marketplace. This book provides excellent living examples to learn from and pray about. Best of all, we're exhorted and encouraged to be *doers* in our marketplace as God leads."

Norm Miller, chairman, Interstate Batteries
and Providence Entertainment, author of *Beyond the Norm*

"Woven into the fabric of these personal stories is the theme of joy that comes with sharing the good news in our daily lives. The messages of hope, courage, and love have never been more important or more relevant than they are today."

Byron J. Bailey, M.D., FACS, past president,
American Academy of Otolaryngology-Head and Neck Surgery

"This book proves you don't have to keep your spiritual life out of your business life. There is a take your daughter/son to work day—why not a take God to work day? Why not every day?"

Mark Fletcher, president, ENT Division, Medtronic Xomed

"At a time in our nation's history when ethical behavior and values-based leadership are proving profoundly essential, Christopher Crane and Mike Hamel present thoughts and observations from leaders who practice ethics and win in the marketplace."

Jim Amos, CEO of Mailboxes Etc.

EXECUTIVE Influence

Impacting Your Workplace for Christ

Christopher A. Crane

and

Mike Hamel

NAVPRESS

Bringing Truth to Life
P.O. Box 35001, Colorado Springs, Colorado 80935

OUR GUARANTEE TO YOU

The Navigators is an international Christian organization. Our mission is to reach, disciple, and equip people to know Christ and to make Him known through successive generations. We envision multitudes of diverse people in the United States and every other nation who have a passionate love for Christ, live a lifestyle of sharing Christ's love, and multiply spiritual laborers among those without Christ.

NavPress is the publishing ministry of The Navigators. NavPress publications help believers learn biblical truth and apply what they learn to their lives and ministries. Our mission is to stimulate spiritual formation among our readers.

© 2003 by Mike Hamel and Christopher A. Crane
All rights reserved. No part of this publication may be reproduced in any form without written permission from NavPress, P.O. Box 35001, Colorado Springs, CO 80935.
www.navpress.com

ISBN 1-57683-373-9

Cover design and photo by The Envoy Group
Creative Team: Kent Wilson, Greg Clouse, Darla Hightower

Unless otherwise identified, all Scripture quotations in this publication are taken from the HOLY BIBLE: NEW INTERNATIONAL VERSION® (NIV®). Copyright © 1973, 1978, 1984 by International Bible Society. Used by permission of Zondervan Publishing House. All rights reserved. Also quoted is the New American Standard Bible (NASB), © The Lockman Foundation 1960, 1962, 1963, 1968, 1971, 1972, 1973, 1975, 1977.

The authors of this book have provided anecdotal narratives of different experiences and successes with incorporating spirituality in their business ventures. Any individual interested in adopting this type of motivational approach should seek experienced legal counsel to address the propriety of such methods under applicable state and federal law. **THE VIEWS, IDEAS AND SUGGESTIONS EXPRESSED HEREIN ARE SOLELY THOSE OF THE INDIVIDUAL AUTHORS AND SHOULD NOT BE CONSIDERED RECOMMENDATIONS OF NAVPRESS, WHO EXPRESSLY DISCLAIMS ANY LIABILITY RESULTING THEREFROM.**

Library of Congress Cataloging-in-Publication Data
Crane, Christopher A., 1951-
Executive influence : impacting your workplace for Christ / Christopher A. Crane and Mike Hamel.
    p. cm.
    ISBN 1-57683-373-9
1. Witness bearing (Christianity) 2. Business--Religious aspects--Christianity. I. Hamel, Mike. II. Title.
BV4520.C695 2003
248.8'8--dc21

                                                    2003008330

Printed in the United States of America
1 2 3 4 5 6 7 8 9 10 / 07 06 05 04 03

FOR A FREE CATALOG OF NAVPRESS BOOKS & BIBLE STUDIES,
CALL 1-800-366-7788 (USA) OR 1-416-499-4615 (CANADA)

To my wife, Jane, and our son, Andrew, whose
caring love has always influenced me.
Christopher A. Crane

To Mike Haddorff, a good friend who has had a
great influence on many lives, including mine.
Mike Hamel

Contents

Most Christians are called to the marketplace as their sphere of service to God. Executives like Bill Pollard, former CEO and current chairman of the executive committee of the board of The ServiceMaster Company, are as passionate about their calling as any pastor or missionary.

Christian compassion is often shown through a church or nonprofit organization. But sometimes a for-profit business can be the best avenue to service, as Paul and Terry Klaassen, founders of one of America's largest eldercare providers, have discovered.

God's reputation is impacted by the way His people live their lives and perform their jobs. No one knows this better than builder David Weekley, whose billion-dollar homebuilding company enjoys a 93 percent customer approval rating.

Given the rewards of commitment and the risks of concealment, Ken Eldred, cofounder of Inmac and Ariba Technologies, thinks the biggest mistake Christians can make is remaining quiet about their faith.

"The credibility I gain by how I do my job gives me opportunities to share my faith at work and in the community," says Dale Gifford, chief executive of the second largest benefits consulting company on the planet. "I have to be careful not to underutilize these openings."

Christians who start their own companies are able to determine the profile given to personal faith. In the case of Ray Berryman, founder and CEO of Berryman & Henigar Enterprises, it's front and center.

Accepting those who are "different" demonstrates the life-changing power of the gospel. "Just look at the life of Jesus," says Donna Auguste, cofounder of Freshwater Software. "Christianity was born because of how He reached out to folks without requiring them to change first."

John Beckett, chairman and CEO of The R. W. Beckett Corporation, exemplifies the believer's call to be an ambassador for Christ. "Our assignment is to make a difference wherever we are sent," he says, "including the workplace."

"Ninety percent of those in business believe their purpose is to make money," says Dennis Bakke, cofounder and CEO of The AES Corporation. "I say no." There is a much higher calling — the stewardship of God's resources.

Christians in high-tech environments can help others find a calmness in the chaos that comes from knowing Christ. Greg Newman, cofounder of C2B Technologies, lives and works among people who have dismissed the church as irrelevant.

Many businesses start out as family affairs. When the family is Christian, the company can become an expression of their faith, hope, and love, as it has with Doug and Edward Hawkins Jr. of Litehouse Foods.

Whether running his business or serving as chairman of the Greater Dallas Chamber of Commerce, Albert Black Jr. knows what he's doing—and why. Rising from the projects, his success gives him the chance to share Christ with thousands of people.

Dr. David Parsons, a former Air Force "Top Gun" and a world-renowned pediatric surgeon, tells how Christians in vocations like law and medicine can use their unique opportunities to pass along the good news.

"I don't understand how a Christian can be in business and not have God at the core," says Anne Beiler, founder of Auntie Anne's Pretzels. "If you are a Christian, God is with you. How can you not take Him to work?"

Chapter Fifteen   **Crisis Management**

Believers are to bring hope to the hurting, and thousands did so in the wake of September 11, including Merrill Oster, founder of Oster Communications. "God speaks through crises," Merrill says, "and we should see such times as chances to get serious with Him."

Foreword

It has been said that the next great movement in Christianity is *demonstration*. If we want people to believe in Jesus Christ, then we Christians must behave differently. Gandhi has been quoted as saying that if Christians lived their lives according to the teachings of Jesus, "we all would become Christians." If Christianity is worth anything, then why is the divorce rate among Christians no better than among nonChristians? If Christianity is worth anything, then why are so many supposed Christian leaders running organizations that have gotten morally and ethically off track? These organizations are set up so that the money, recognition, and power move up the hierarchy away from the people doing all the work with the customers. Self-serving leadership seems to be the rule while the servant leadership that Jesus advocated is the exception.

Work would be so much different if more of us in leadership and management positions asked ourselves, "What would Jesus do?" before we acted. While we have to demonstrate our faith through our works, I am not advocating "good works" as the way to relate to God and our fellow man. Tony Evans, the great Dallas preacher, highlighted the balance of faith and works when he said, "Faith gets you to heaven, but it's your works that bring heaven back to earth."

Striking this balance in the workplace is what this book is about. It contains the collective wisdom of more than fifty executives and professionals who are sharing their Christian faith and "walking the talk" in the marketplace. People like Bill Pollard from ServiceMaster, who has been instrumental in ensuring that the company keeps its commitment "to honor God in all we do." And communications expert Merrill Oster, who insists, "If I can create (by my example) a culture where people feel comfortable talking about the real issues of life and how faith applies to them, that's powerful."

This is the book many of us Christians have been waiting for. It brings our faith down to earth 24/7. As Chris and Mike contend, the sound advice of these leaders "in being salt and light in the marketplace" is applicable to all believers, no matter their position or job titles.

When I was writing *The Power of Ethical Management* with the legendary positive-thinking minister Norman Vincent Peale, I asked him if I should quit my business of teaching, consulting, and writing and go back to divinity school. He was quick to reply, "Absolutely not! You have an important congregation in the marketplace and we just don't have enough good preachers there." If Norman could have read *Executive Influence*, he would have been thrilled because it is filled with the thinking of some of the best marketplace preachers available anywhere.

Thanks, Chris and Mike, for creating such a great read that will help us all demonstrate to others that Jesus can be the most influential executive of all. As the faith-driven executives you have interviewed suggest, the only competitive measure that really counts is the width of Jesus' smile when we meet Him in the kingdom and He says, "A job well done, my good and faithful servant."

Ken Blanchard, coauthor,
The One-Minute Manager® and *Leadership by the Book*

Preface

Business executives have a powerful effect on the lives of all Americans. They exert a moral influence on their peers, investors, employees, and customers — for good or ill. And for those who are Christians, there is an added spiritual impact that can count for eternity.

This book is written for believers who serve Christ in the marketplace. It contains the collective wisdom of more than fifty executives and professionals who have at least three things in common: (1) they are evangelical Christians; (2) they are in leadership positions; and (3) they are living out their faith in a variety of ways, such as:

- Sharing the gospel with those around them.
- Creating and maintaining faith-friendly corporate cultures.
- Modeling high ethical standards in how they do business.
- Investing company and personal resources in worthy causes.
- Using their influence to promote spiritual renewal in America.

None of the contributors volunteered to be part of this book. We sought them out because of their reputations for being Christians who have proven themselves outstanding executives. Their personal integrity and business acumen have won them the respect of their peers, Christian and nonChristian alike. Their sound advice on being salt and light in the marketplace is applicable to all believers, no matter their positions or job titles.

A few executives stand out as role models in our own lives. Merrill Oster has been a great example of a Christian entrepreneur and CEO. Steve James has been a model of a caring Christian while serving on the board of COMPS InfoSystems, Inc.

Our thanks to all the busy entrepreneurs and executives we spoke with for their time and candor. Our thanks to Marcella Radovich and Karen Velton for their invaluable help in taping and transcribing the interviews. And our special thanks to Jesus Christ, the most influential executive of all.

Christopher A. Crane
Mike Hamel

Chapter One

Service Call

Most Christians are called to the marketplace as their sphere of service to God. Even in Jesus' day only a few disciples left their jobs to devote themselves exclusively to the gospel. The vast majority of believers, then and now, dispense salt in daily doses while earning a living in the world. What a high and holy calling, says University of Southern California philosophy professor Dallas Willard:

> Possession and direction of the forces of wealth are as legitimate an expression of the redemptive rule of God in human life as is Bible teaching or a prayer meeting. For example, it is as great and as difficult a spiritual calling to run the factories and the mines, the banks and the department stores, the schools and government agencies for the Kingdom of God as it is to pastor a church or serve as an evangelist. There truly is no division between sacred and secular except what we have created. And that is why the division of the legitimate roles and functions of human life into the sacred and the secular does incalculable damage to our individual lives and to the cause of Christ. Holy

people must stop going into "church work" as their natural course of action and take up holy orders in farming, industry, law, education, banking, and journalism with the same zeal previously given to evangelism or to pastoral and missionary work.[1]

We must be careful not to assume, however, that different spheres of ministry mean different kinds of ministry. Evangelism, encouragement, teaching, and service are not restricted to church settings. Spiritual gifts can have more impact during the week than on weekends. Executives like Bill Pollard, former CEO and current chairman of the executive committee of the board of The ServiceMaster Company, are as confident about their callings and as devoted to their ministries as any pastor or missionary.

ServiceMaster was founded over fifty years ago by Marion Wade, a devout Christian. Today the company employs or manages a quarter-million people in forty-five countries and serves more than twelve million customers annually. ServiceMaster recruited Pollard from his position as professor and administrator at Wheaton College in 1977. On his watch the firm has been recognized by *Fortune* as the number one service company among the Fortune 500. *Financial Times* recently acknowledged Service-Master as one of the most respected companies in the world. This respect is due not just to their scale—annual revenues in excess of seven billion dollars—but to their commitment to honoring God in the process.

Respect all human beings as God's image-bearers.

"We've got a job to do here," says Pollard, "but that doesn't mean we have to ignore faith, or God. As a business we strive to excel at generating profits and creating value for our shareholders. If we don't want to play by these rules we don't belong in the game. However, we also believe we can help shape the human character at the same time. We can be an open community where questions of spiritual development, the existence of God, and a person's relationship to Him are issues for discussion and even debate. We try to encourage people to ask, 'If I have a spiritual side, what is it? If there is a God, what is my relationship to Him?'"

From the very beginning the leadership at ServiceMaster has recognized the importance of dealing with the whole person, which includes the physical, the intellectual, and the spiritual. This latter dimension comes from being made in God's image, a belief that finds expression among the company's twenty-one principles of leadership, one of which states, "We have all been created in God's image, and the results of our leadership will be measured beyond the workplace."

In the business of managing time, money, and people, it's essential that spirituality be step one, agrees Tom Chappell, CEO of Tom's of Maine:

> Spirituality says the world is bigger than our balance sheet, bigger than the walls of Tom's of Maine. . . . Setting this value out in our mission gives people in the company permission to use their whole selves—to have more than just their minds or hands on their work, but also their souls and their spirits. We try to be open to the head, heart, and the hands here. The more people are freed up to be their best selves, the easier it becomes for them to provide our customers with good products, our owners with good rates of return, and our community with a sensitive, responsible corporate partner.[2]

ServiceMaster's track record illustrates that there doesn't have to be a tension between honoring God and financial performance. These two components are part of the company's now-famous four business values:

> To honor God in all we do,
> To help people develop,
> To pursue excellence,
> To grow profitably.

These values are published prominently in ServiceMaster's annual reports and engraved in a marble wall outside their corporate headquarters. "Few people find fault with our commitment to a set of principles," Pollard writes in his bestselling book *The Soul of the Firm*. "Quite frankly, it is the 'God language' that raises eyebrows. 'Aren't you walking on shaky ground when you try to mix God and profits?' ask the critics. 'And what about employees who don't choose to believe the way you do? Aren't you forcing your beliefs on them?'"[3]

"Spirituality isn't synonymous with Christianity," Pollard explains. "We encourage spirituality and faith in relationship to work and life, but this doesn't create what could be called a Christian environment. Sure, there are Bible studies at ServiceMaster, but people initiate them, not the company. We also have Muslims who pray at work five times a day, as do most large corporations. Faith may be expressed in various ways here. I accept those who have a different kind of faith. I accept those who disagree with me. My faith is not the company's faith; it's personal. No corporation can make my decisions for me. If you are curious about my faith, examine my life.

"As a follower of Jesus Christ, I'm concerned with how I touch the spiritual side of people within my business. Do I use my leadership to try to impose or propagate my faith? Or, do I seek to live it in ways that can be examined by my colleagues and, yes, even be embraced by some, within the context of working together to produce goods and services and generate a profit? I have chosen the latter approach, and it has consumed much of my time and attention."

Bruce Duncan, former vice president of Investor Relations at ServiceMaster, shares Pollard's commitment, yet has followed it in a different direction, taking early retirement in his mid-forties to enter a church-planting program. "When I was hired in 1990," Duncan recalls, "I talked with Bill about my long-term plans. At one time he had been a Sunday school teacher of mine and I knew him well. He understood my dream and while he gave me wonderful opportunities to advance, he never pressured me to stay. My ten years at ServiceMaster were very enjoyable and productive. They've provided me a measure of financial freedom as company stock did exceptionally well in the 1990s. I also gained an understanding of what most people go through in their daily lives. Few pastors have this because they haven't worked in the business world."

Show and tell, don't push and preach.

While striving to create a faith-friendly environment, Pollard has not viewed his executive position as a platform from which to preach. "I have seen it as a great opportunity to demonstrate my faith," he says, "a faith that affects how I make business decisions. It affects how I integrate my family into my work and how I live out the biblical principles of truth, caring, honesty, and love in a marketplace environment. The God of my faith is the God of the Bible, a personal God who has created the people with whom I work, with whom I compete—people I sometimes dislike and whom I also love. I believe that God has invested each one of them with dignity, worth, potential, and freedom to choose. My daily challenge has been not just to talk about my faith, but to live it in the way I recognize and treat others, including those who do not agree with me. In the words of our founder, Marion Wade, 'if I don't live it, I don't believe it.'"

Pollard, a stickler for clear thinking and correct terminology, has a problem with words like influence and platform, because they convey an underlying assumption that leaders can use their positions to impose their beliefs on others. He prefers less imposing words like sharing or relating. This kind of show-and-tell life is much more demanding than simply pontificating from an executive platform. "Christians in positions of authority have to monitor their actions to make sure that what they say and do is consistent with their stated faith," says Pollard. "I find myself from time to time seeking forgiveness from people because I have acted or spoken in a way that was inconsistent with my faith. At the same time, one of the exciting things to me is being in situations where my words or conduct turn people on about Christianity. I've had people come to my office and accept Christ as their Savior. I've had the same experience while traveling. When the Spirit is at work, the opportunities are there, but one has to be careful not to proceed based on position. The cross provides a level playing field in the process of God's drawing people to Himself, namely that we are all sinners."

Care for your people the way Jesus did for His.

It's not surprising that the former CEO of ServiceMaster believes one of the best ways for Christian leaders to share their faith is to serve others. Servant leadership reflects the example set by Jesus Himself as He took a towel and washed His disciples' feet. In so doing, He taught that no leader is greater than the people he or she leads, and that even the humblest task is not beneath a leader. "The kings of the Gentiles lord it over them," Jesus said, "and those who exercise authority over them call themselves Benefactors. But you are not to be like that. Instead, the greatest among you should be like the youngest, and the one who rules like the one who serves" (Luke 22:25-26).

No matter the profession, Pollard insists the duty of every Christian is to "learn what Jesus did and try to imitate the pattern of His life. While He never pulled any punches, Jesus was always in the process of seeking people to accept Him. The Scripture says we are His ambassadors with a message of reconciliation, and to be effective we need to better understand our faith. This requires study and continual reflection upon God's Word. That's always been my fundamental starting point. I also think an understanding of the history of Christianity is important because there's much we can learn from it."

One doesn't reach the top of his or her chosen profession without a single-minded approach to life. Pollard's intensity is immediately apparent to anyone who meets him. However, his focus isn't on business per se. "My one priority is seeking and serving the Lord I love. He has called me to be a witness and a servant in all I do. At times this will have me intensely focused on business, and other times absorbed in my family, and still other times wrapped up in church or some other activity. The issue is not to put these responsibilities in juxtaposition so much as it is to ask: Is Christ in it? What does He want me to do?"

That question is at the heart of Christianity. "Lord, what would you have me to do?" The "where" aspect will vary from person to person, but the "how" aspect will always involve service. Whether from the boardroom of a multibillion-dollar corporation—as in Pollard's case—or from the maintenance department, how we serve should draw favorable attention to whom we serve.

Other Voices

A number of years ago I changed my title to Chief Spiritual Officer (of The Ken Blanchard Companies), making it part of my job to keep the energy and spirit up among our staff of 250. One thing I do is a morning devotional on voice mail. Initially some people resented it. They suspected me of trying to push religion on them. So I made a deal with them. If I planned to get really Christian, I'd say so up front so they could turn it off if they didn't want to listen.

Ken Blanchard, coauthor of *The One-Minute Manager*

I don't believe Christian executives should use their positions as platforms from which to preach to their employees or peers. Rather, they should share through the example of their lives. If executives would simply follow two rules, they would have plenty of opportunities to demonstrate the difference Christian belief makes. Rule one, don't duck; rule two, don't impose.

Bob Buford, author of *Halftime and Game Plan*

YOUR TURN

Post a weekly voice mail or e-mail to your staff. Share a spiritual or inspirational thought that will encourage them or challenge their thinking. Be open and personable, not official. Depending on your personality and communication style, you can share what God is teaching you or include quotes from books or articles you have enjoyed. Invite people to respond to you if they have questions.

Chapter Two

The Business of True Religion

C hristians have always shown the love of Christ by serving those in need. Collectively this is often done through a church, charity, or nonprofit organization. But sometimes creating a for-profit company can be the best venue for service. It is a simplistic assumption that for-profit businesses are only interested in making money. Many believers are called to a business context, and their labor is as vital as what's done in a church or charitable setting. Indeed, some Christians are much more fruitful and have far more impact precisely because they are in business. Case in point: Paul and Terry Klaassen, founders of Sunrise Assisted Living, one of America's largest eldercare providers.

"During the twentieth century, the number of Americans aged sixty-five and older increased eleven-fold from three million to thirty-three million," report Leona and Richard Bergstrom, authors of *Amazing Grays*. "According to U.S. Census Bureau projections, that number will more than double in the next four decades to well over seventy million!"[1] Because almost seven million of these seniors require some form of physical assistance to live with dignity, a whole new service industry has developed to meet this expanding need.

Obey the call to full-time ministry, even if it means starting a business.

Sunrise Assisted Living is the Klaassens' response to this need and their answer to a call to ministry. As a teenager, Terry Merritt came face-to-face with the crisis in eldercare when she and her father cared for her terminally ill mother at home rather than move her to a nursing home. Later, after she married Paul Klaassen, the couple volunteered at several senior-care facilities. What they saw troubled them. It also motivated them to sell their home and borrow $25,000 so they could buy and renovate an abandoned nursing home. They designed an elegant environment, developed a resident-centered operating model, and moved in to take care of the first residents themselves. Soon they had a full house of thirty-three seniors and the prototype for what would become a multimillion-dollar business.

The Sunrise name came from a kitchen table discussion before the first home was purchased. "We had already rejected the typical retirement center names like Last Gasp or Shady Acres," Terry says wryly. "My stepmother left the table and returned with a Bible. She read Luke 1:78-79, which says, 'Because of the tender mercy of our God, with which the Sunrise from on high shall visit us, to shine upon those who sit in darkness and the shadow of death, to guide our feet into the way of peace' (NASB). That was it! Sunrise would be about taking people out of the gloom that characterized the nursing homes we had seen and giving them a way of peace."

Paul and Terry had seen the dark side of eldercare firsthand. They had also observed a more dignified approach with Paul's relatives in Holland, which they used as a model. Word of their resident-centered, compassionate care began to spread. Demand grew, and they opened two more homes in the mid-1980s and a couple new homes each year thereafter. By 1994 they had twenty assisted living communities, and in 1996 they took Sunrise public.

Being the CEO of a successful company isn't what Paul expected to be doing with his life. "I became a follower of Jesus Christ in college," he recounts. "I started a Christian rock band in the 1970s and eventually married the alto vocalist [Terry]. After our music days were over, I applied and was accepted to two seminaries. I was on my way to becoming a pastor when I decided I wanted to do eldercare instead, and mainly because I saw this work as a ministry."

"To this day I don't think of it much differently," Paul told *Assisted Living Success* magazine. "Some people have said, 'Wow, what a shift!' The real calling of faith is defined as the caring for orphans and widows in their distress. I chose a little different approach, but I still consider it a ministry."[2]

The word ministry means "service," and the Klaassens have chosen to serve seniors with the zeal of pastors caring for their flocks. *Forbes* once described Paul as, "An intense . . . evangelical Christian (who) tries to infuse every management decision at Sunrise Assisted Living with a healthy dose of God. . . . Printed on the back of the Klaassens' business cards are their principles of service, which include 'nurturing the spirit' and 'preserving dignity.'"[3] Sunrise's foundational value is defined as, "Belief in the Sacred Value of Human Life."

Paul smiles when he says, "In most articles written about Sunrise the first thing they point out is our Christian faith and principles. We are often identified in this way and I'm delighted because this is who we are. To me the worldview articulated by Jesus Christ is the one that best answers the questions about the human condition. It makes the most sense as I look at the alternatives. I try to live my life in a way that is consistent with this worldview, which includes how I use my position as a CEO."

Terry shares Paul's perspective. "I have tried to maintain a consistent approach to life, whether it was in school or in my jobs before Sunrise. As a Christian my faith is the foundation on which I make my decisions and form relationships. This came out strongly when I functioned as the chief operating officer of Sunrise, hiring people, training them, and setting expectations for them."

Accept the downside, and upside, of going public with your faith.

In many ways successful entrepreneurs and executives are arguably as influential as elected officials. They have platforms in society; people pay attention to them. But these positions of influence come with certain disadvantages as well. One is that people notice if they stumble. Another is that the scope of their influence only occasionally translates into individual spiritual conversions. People are often drawn to a commitment of faith through a relationship with someone. Because of the demands on their time, top executives have relatively few deep relationships.

An additional risk of high-profile faith is that it makes Christians an easy target for the jaded press. "Christian executives must not be afraid of the world's cynicism and the media's twisting of our faith," says Terry. "An article appeared in one of the big business magazines a while back that really angered me. It insinuated that we used our faith to manipulate people to move into our homes. To be maligned for genuinely trying to live out your faith is a risk that Christians must accept. But it's not easy. I have to challenge myself to be more bold about my faith without worrying if I will be misunderstood."

On the positive side of the ledger, Paul stresses that CEOs play the major role in affecting a corporation's culture. They shape its values and vision. They manage the hiring process. They decide what to highlight and what to downplay. They also have influence in the communities where they do business. However, Paul warns, "Trying to use an executive position as a platform from which to preach like a pastor is unwise. The fragrance of our faith will be evident in how we live, how we conduct business, and how we love others.

"But that's not to say we should be silent and withdrawn," he continues. "I have rarely seen Christian executives make the mistake of being too passionate about their faith. Almost everyone likes passion. If it's okay for me to be passionate about the Redskins or the Orioles, why in the world can't I be passionate about other things in life? I see so few people being bold, while so many—myself included at times—are privatized to the point of having no impact. I'd love to see faith get to the level of the weather or sports in our everyday conversations.

"I have never really taken any flak for being a Christian. It makes me wonder if I am enough in the game. Christian executives are too timid. We are so afraid of offending somebody that we've become neutered. But these fears are misplaced. CEOs and business leaders, too, often think they are under the same restrictions as schoolteachers. A schoolteacher may be prohibited from putting the Ten Commandments on the wall or singing Christian songs at Christmas, but business leaders have far more latitude. The federal courts have consistently ruled that the threshold for a business to watch out for is harassment, not faith. I know very few Christians who come even remotely close to crossing that line. Businesses are not schools. They can, and should, create work environments that are faith-friendly."

From the beginning, Sunrise has maintained such an atmosphere. "We have many natural openings to discuss spirituality and faith in our work," Terry explains. "Eldercare is all about being with people at the end of their lives. And if this is not a time to talk about faith and God, when is? However, our role is not to push our faith on anyone but rather to serve them. That's what Christ calls us to do, to give whatever support is needed.

"Near the end of life the spiritual needs of our clients are just as legitimate as their physical and emotional needs and should be addressed. Each of our homes have connections with local churches and synagogues in order to provide worship services. In some regions there are interdenominational chaplains available. We are very sensitive about what could be viewed as proselytizing or creating alignments with any particular churches, but this doesn't mean we should ignore a very important part of people's lives."

Use your resources to foster spiritual growth, inside your company and out.

Sunrise takes this same faith-inclusive approach to their staff. "If prospective employees are acquainted with the history of Sunrise," Terry points out, "they know beforehand they will be working for an organization with Christian founders who are comfortable including faith as a part of how we do business. We are very up-front about this. We certainly don't limit our hiring to Christians; we just hire people with servant hearts."

One way Sunrise fosters the development of personal faith is through the "wellness program" in effect at corporate headquarters. Everyone gets $500 a year that can only be spent on wellness. The money can be used to quit smoking, to join a health club, or to attend a spiritual event. "This gives us a practical way to encourage spiritual activity," Paul says. "Is there a chance someone will go to a Buddhist monastery? Yes, and this wouldn't bother me."

In addition to creating a faith-friendly environment, the Klaassens are busy trying to influence the culture outside Sunrise as well. Terry is an active member of The Committee of 200, a leadership group of select corporate women in the United States, and a member of the International Women's Forum. Paul is the chairman of The Trinity Forum, a group that engages leaders on the key issues of their personal and public lives in the context of faith. "We are Christian in commitment," Paul clarifies, "but we welcome people of all faiths who are interested in our programs. We try to introduce leaders to the big ideas that have shaped our civilization and to the faith that has led to its highest achievements."

One of the "big ideas" Paul has been trying to get across for the last twenty years is that there should be no difference between Sunday and the rest of the week. "I want to encourage people not to be schizophrenic," he says. "Americans have compartmentalized faith into a few hours of the week, and this privatization of spirituality has had a very negative impact on our country."

Part of what has been lost for many by this segmentation is the realization of work as vocation. As Robert Banks, executive director of the De Pree Leadership Center, puts it:

> There has been a profound shift from following a call or vocation to pursuing a career. Whenever someone has a strong sense of vocation, it forms a bridge between religious beliefs and public activities. This sense of vocation enables faith to be carried more fully into one's conduct at work and into workplace structures. When the emphasis shifts from calling to career, however, the link between a person's private (Sunday) and public (Monday-Friday) worlds is weakened. Work becomes a personal expression rather than a divine commission, a

means of personal achievement rather than of public obedience, an arena for individual fulfillment rather than social transformation.[4]

Paul and Terry have followed their sense of divine commission into the business of true religion. Their success in serving others has given them the credibility and capital to become agents of social transformation. The light from Sunrise is not only brightening the last days of many seniors and their families, it's exposing the fallacy of compartmentalized faith.

"You are the light of the world," Jesus told His disciples. "A city on a hill cannot be hidden. Neither do people light a lamp and put it under a bowl. Instead they put it on its stand, and it gives light to everyone in the house. In the same way, let your light shine before men, that they may see your good deeds and praise your Father in heaven" (Matthew 5:14-16).

For the Klaassens, shining the light is what Sunrise is all about.

Other Voices

I'm in the trucking business and after I became a Christian I put a picture of a church on the back of our trailers with the words, "Start the week off right: Attend the church of your choice." I have received hundreds of letters from people saying how much this little reminder has meant to them. I also have a phrase on the back of my business card that reads, "If we meet and you forget me, you have lost a friend; but if you meet Jesus Christ and forget Him, you have lost everything." These words constantly remind me to tell others what life is really about.

Roger Roberson, chairman of Roberson Transportation Services

When you own a motor vehicle dealership everyone assumes you're a crook. If you quote a fair price to customers, they don't believe you. Some salespeople get frustrated when you won't use underhanded tactics. The trouble is, these tactics are what everybody expects. But we let our yes be yes and our no be no. We choose to be different, especially since our name publicly represents the Savior. When people ask, "Where did you get Morning Star?" I tell them about the passages in the Bible. I tell them my Savior is the bright Morning Star.

Doug Abbotts, CEO of Morning Star Mobility, Inc.

YOUR TURN

Work on becoming a good listener. Even if it doesn't come naturally, do it by discipline. Every time you talk with someone, condition yourself to ask (in the quiet of your mind if not out loud), "What can I do to be useful to you?" Then do it if you can, without fanfare or grandstanding. Such good works may open up a chance to share the good news.

Chapter Three
Built to Last

J esus of Nazareth was a carpenter for most of His adult life. Later, as an itinerant preacher, He often used illustrations from the building trade, as in this well-known passage from Matthew 7. "Therefore everyone who hears these words of mine and puts them into practice is like a wise man who built his house on the rock. The rain came down, the streams rose, and the winds blew and beat against that house; yet it did not fall, because it had its foundation on the rock" (verses 24-25).

Building on the foundation of Jesus Christ means to live according to His teachings. Such a life will survive the test of time and bring glory to the Master Builder.

All contractors know the value of a good name and the liability of a bad one. As craftspeople, they will be judged by their work, not their words—by what they produce, not what they promise. Advertising can be bought, but a good reputation has to be earned.

God's reputation in the world is affected by how Christians live. Profession is not as important as performance. Salvation is not by works, but it leads to works, according to the apostle Paul: "It is by grace you have been saved, through faith . . . not by works, so that no one can boast. For we are God's workmanship, created in Christ Jesus *to do good works*, which God prepared in advance for us to do" (Ephesians 2:8-10, emphasis added).

The desire to do good—meaning both high quality and virtuous work—should be foundational for every Christian. This passion certainly fuels the fires of David Weekley. The company that bears his name is currently the second largest privately owned homebuilder in America, with sales nearing a billion dollars and a customer satisfaction rating of 93 percent. Over the past twenty-five years Weekley Homes has won hundreds of awards for excellence and was the first company to earn the three most coveted awards in their industry: America's Best Builder, National Builder of the Year (twice), and the National Housing Quality Award.

Don't presume on a "Christian" label to build your business.

David is the product of a godly home. He became a Christian at a Young Life camp and was active in the organization during high school. After college he went to work for a Houston builder as a management trainee. Eighteen months into the job they changed the compensation structure from what they had originally stated. He wrote a letter to the president about what he considered an unethical move—and promptly lost his job. That's when his brother suggested they start their own company. David had married his high school sweetheart just a month before getting fired. They lived off her teacher's salary as Weekley Homes began building single-family houses. By 1984 they were putting up six hundred units annually.

From the outset, David's faith has been evident in his work ethic and his company policies. However, he doesn't use the Christian label to create leverage. He doesn't advertise as a Christian business. He doesn't place ads on Christian radio or in the various Christian business directories. "Our success can't be based on having a certain tag," he insists. "It has to come from the quality of what we do. It has to come from doing the right thing regardless of the cost or consequences. For example, we once spent $2 million on repiping five hundred homes when we learned the pipe wouldn't hold up over time. We didn't know whether the manufacturer would pay us back or not. We have to take initiatives like this to maintain our reputation for quality."

This emphasis on quality is more than a strategy to secure market share. It grows out of David's desire to make a difference in people's lives and is expressed in the company vision statement: Enhancing People's Lives: Our Team, Our Customers and Our Community. "A home is more than sticks and bricks," David emphasizes, "so having our team see that they are enhancing our customers' lives is significant. Everyone wants to find a higher sense of meaning in their work than just earning a paycheck. For me this has a Christian connotation; for others it doesn't. Still, I think everyone wants to believe that their work matters."

"The best of them [executives] understand that what really motivates people is something higher than just materialism and dealing with their own little egos," says Joseph Jaworski, former head of Global Scenario Planning for the Royal Dutch/Shell Group. "What really motivates the most creative people is to have their values and their search for meaning aligned with corporate values."[1]

That David has been able to accomplish his vision of blessing people—to use a biblical word—is affirmed by his company's repeated appearance on *Fortune's* list of the 100 Best Companies to Work For.

Include spiritual help in your benefits package.

To help team members grow as people, Weekley Homes has hired Marketplace Ministries to provide company chaplains. There's no doubt in David's tone when he says, "Of all the things we've done in our Employee Assistance Program, from 401(k)s to profit sharing to medical benefits, nowhere have we've gotten more bang for our buck than with Marketplace Ministries. The stories I hear are amazing. I remember a lady in one of our offices telling me how the chaplain showed up two hours after she'd been served divorce papers at work. Her comment to me was, 'He saved my life!'"

For a few dollars a month per team member, the chaplains have done funerals and weddings and everything in between, including being nonjudgmental listeners when someone wants to talk. Weekley Homes operates in fourteen cities from Colorado to the Carolinas and the chaplains are available weekly at each location. "Hiring chaplains on a subcontracting basis makes a lot of sense for a widely dispersed operation like ours," says David. "It's a great deal; every business ought to be doing it. If the U.S. military recognizes the need to have chaplains, why don't more companies?"

Some companies do see the need. "Ever since Austaco Inc., the sixth largest Pizza Hut and Taco Bell franchisee in the U.S., began hiring chaplains in 1992 through . . . Marketplace Ministries, the company has reduced its annual turnover from 300 percent to 125 percent. In fast-food time, that's like having workers stay on for an eternity. The company credits the chaplain program for the drop."[2]

Jesus said, "It is more blessed to give than receive," and David is learning to share the blessing. He admits that he used to pressure his people to work harder so he would have more money and time to give away. A few years ago all that changed. "I came to realize this was pretty selfish. We've since started a company outreach program wherein each team comes up with various charitable activities they want to do. It might be building a home for Habitat for Humanity or remodeling an elderly person's home, or something else within our realm of expertise. They do the work and I fund the project."

Incorporating the spiritual dimension into Weekley Homes has been a gradual process that has run parallel with the growth of David Weekley himself. "I've changed as I've grown in my faith," he acknowledges. "I was a lot harder person in my late twenties and early thirties. God continues to work on me and I am more compassionate as a boss now. I'm also more aware of my responsibility as a role model in the company and the community. I try to act in Christlike ways without pounding people over the head with the Bible."

A few instances along the way have made David more careful. "I remember one Christmas when I gave a book on Christian business wisdom to senior management. I later found out that one of my newly hired executives was Jewish. He took offense and returned the book along with a note. He has since left the company and I felt badly about putting him in an awkward situation. But at the same time I know I can't remain silent. I'm trying to be more open about my faith in the right settings. At our annual meeting this year I talked about why we exist as a company. I used a couple of stories from the Bible like the parable of the talents. I let the team members and their spouses know that this is where our strong moral foundation comes from. Others might buy into it for different reasons, but my motivation comes from my faith. This was the first time I've been so direct. I'm learning and stretching when it comes to sharing publicly."

Invest yourself in things that matter more than worldly success.

Weekley Homes was building six hundred homes a year in 1984 when the bottom fell out of the market. Housing starts in Houston dropped from thirty thousand to six thousand in six months. Recalling those dark days, David says, "Most companies went broke, but we expanded in to Dallas and that market pulled us through. That was a very challenging time for us; still, I was enjoying life in the fast lane. I was the president of the local builder's association at thirty years old and saw myself as God's gift to the homebuilding industry. I got caught up in the run for success. I traveled a lot and routinely put in eighty-hour weeks. Eventually I reached the end of my rope and considered selling the company."

David got help from three men at this critical point. His brother Dick helped him see the need to bring in someone to handle day-to-day operations. They hired John Johnson as executive vice president and the company has grown in ten years from about $200 million in sales to almost a billion. The third helper was Bob Buford, whose book gave David a game plan for the future.

"I picked up *Halftime* at just the right time for me," Weekley says. "I had been in business for eighteen years and was getting burned out. I had always wanted to be successful because of the drive to excel that had been ingrained in me from an early age. But once I achieved financial success, my drive decreased and I began looking for something else."

Because of the influence of *Halftime*, and Stanley Tam's *God Owns My Business*, David decided to keep the company but to change his motivation. "What reinvigorated my interest in business was committing half of what I made to charitable purposes. I got the idea from the church I grew up in, Memorial Drive Presbyterian Church. They have what they call 'dollar for dollar' giving. Every dollar spent inside the church is matched by a dollar spent outside. I decided that for every dollar I made, I would put a dollar into charitable causes. Over the last few years I've been blessed to be able to give back millions of dollars, which has given new meaning to what I'm doing now."

When he committed to give 50 percent of his income away, David also determined to donate 50 percent of his time to the various activities he supported. "It has been rewarding to get plugged into community activities and charitable organizations and to exert a spiritual influence on

Executive Influence

them," he says. "A number of my gifts have been anonymous because I think that's best in most cases. But in some instances I take a more direct approach. For example, I'm involved with a secular camp and I'm talking to them about the need for a chapel and a chaplain, a need that I can help fund. I'm also involved with a private school where we put a strong emphasis on character development. Then there's the hospital that's putting up some new buildings. I'm trying to get them to move the chapel to street level instead of burying it somewhere inside the complex."

David also uses his influence to help worthy causes that aren't as high profile. He works with good ministries that haven't gotten connected to adequate funding because the business community doesn't know them. "As a Christian businessman, I can help an organization like the College of Biblical Studies. It's the largest minority Bible college in the country, yet they have low public visibility. We've formed an advisory group with business leaders who can help them get the funding needed to take the school to the next level."

Ask Weekley if he's arrived and he'll tell you that his character is still under construction. "The whole issue of handling success and money is a challenge I continue to work on. My faith has been developing ever since my mountaintop experience with Christ as a teenager. For a while I was pursuing my activities for my own success rather than on God's behalf. But today I'm paying more attention to how I care for others, invest my resources, and exert my influence. I can honestly say that I'm at a place now where I feel like I've got the right motivations for what I'm doing. I can see myself staying in business and sharing my God-given resources for another twenty-five years."

The foremost church architect once said,

> I laid a foundation as an expert builder, and someone else
> is building on it. But each one should be careful how he

builds. For no one can lay any foundation other than the one already laid, which is Jesus Christ. If any man builds on this foundation using gold, silver, costly stones, wood, hay or straw, his work will be shown for what it is, because the Day will bring it to light. . . . If what he has built survives, he will receive his reward. (1 Corinthians 3:10-14)

Quality work is built to last—for a lifetime and beyond.

Other Voices

Interstate Batteries has a full-time chaplain who is available to pray with and counsel employees, or to direct them to outside resources. We also have a large library of Christian books, tapes, magazines, and videos that can be checked out through the chaplain's office. All new employees receive a Bible on their first day, and voluntary Bible studies are held on the premises before work.

> Norm Miller, chairman of Interstate Batteries of America,
> author of *Beyond the Norm*

A senior computer company executive once spoke to my M.B.A. class. He said that his hard-nosed business approach had landed him a very high position in the company while he was still young. He added that because of a personal experience, he was now producing far better results then he had earlier in his career. A student asked about the experience, so the executive shared his life-changing encounter with Jesus Christ. Students talked about the successful executive and the impact of his presentation for the rest of the year.

> Bruce Fournier, associate professor of business,
> Wilfrid Laurier University

Your Turn

The backs of most business cards are blank. Why not put a provocative phrase in this free space as a conversation starter? Use one of these sayings from recent bumper stickers—or make up your own:

God grades on the cross, not the curve.

God doesn't want shares of your life;
He wants controlling interest.

Man's way leads to a hopeless end.
God's way leads to an endless hope.

Give God what's right, not what's left.

Chapter Four
24/7

C hristianity is a 24/7 calling, to apply a new phrase to an old truth. Jesus cautioned would-be disciples to count the cost before enlisting to make sure they could finish what they started: "Anyone who does not carry his cross and follow me cannot be my disciple. Suppose one of you wants to build a tower. Will he not first sit down and estimate the cost to see if he has enough money to complete it? For if he lays the foundation and is not able to finish it, everyone who sees it will ridicule him, saying, 'This fellow began to build and was not able to finish'" (Luke 14:27-30).

Starting a business is also a demanding, all-consuming undertaking. So what's a believer who wants to be both a committed disciple and a successful entrepreneur to do? It is possible to put God first and run a thriving business at the same time—but it isn't easy. Just ask Ken Eldred. He is the founder or cofounder of such fast-growing technology companies as Inmac and Ariba Technologies, Inc. He has also worked with other well-known businesses including ClickAction, Office Depot, and Norm Thompson Outfitters. In 1988 the Institute of American Entrepreneurs named him Retail Entrepreneur of the Year for the San Francisco Bay Area.

Ken's aggressiveness in business is an expression of his commitment to Christ. "When I became a Christian in 1972," he recalls, "it seemed that too many people were weekend warriors. I had a problem with this attitude. Within six months of becoming a believer, I decided to make Jesus Christ lord of everything, not only Sunday but every day. Becoming a Christian meant I was a new person and I needed to be that person at all times."

Put the Lord first in life and in business and trust Him to take care of the rest.

This full-time commitment is why Ken took his faith to work with him when he started Inmac, the first company to market computer products via catalog. The company soon expanded to other countries and eventually generated annual revenues of $400 million. "We started Inmac with $5,000 and a grocery bag of connector parts," says Eldred with a trace of nostalgia. "I put in forty hours a week, and of course nobody would invest in a company like this because VCs [venture capitalists] want you putting in sixty or seventy hours a week minimum. But I wasn't going to do that. I'd committed to God that He was first; my wife was second, and my kids came next. I told Him that He would have to run the business while I was gone because I could only give it forty hours a week. We were probably one of the few companies that grew to the size we did from so little money and so little investment of the founder's time."

Not that Ken was "letting go and letting God." "It was a very intense forty hours, but when I left, I went home and spent time with my family. God defines success differently from our culture. Success means that my relationship with Him is good and growing. It means that I have a quality relationship with my wife. It means my children know I love them and feel like I'm there for them. And then if the company is prosperous, that's a bonus. Roberta and I have been married over thirty years and neither she nor my three boys have ever felt as if the business came first. That's true success."

Ken's time at work had boundaries, but it wasn't compartmentalized or segregated from the rest of his life. A year after he started Inmac, he asked a pastor how he could make Inmac a Christian company. The wise man told him, "There's no such thing; only people are Christians. But believers can use their businesses as opportunities to make Christ known." This led Ken to put tracts such as *The Four Spiritual Laws* and *Got Life?* in the office lobby, a practice that generated both light and heat. He vividly remembers the day a very angry employee came to his office and loudly complained, "I don't like those tracts! I've been taking them out of the lobby!" "What do you want me to do?" Eldred replied. "You knew they were there before you came to work here, and they will be there as long as I'm president. As we continued to talk she softened and eventually asked, 'How do I become a Christian?'"

Because of that conversation, Ken put a letter in the lobby explaining that the literature didn't represent everyone's views, but it did represent his opinion of what was important in life. He invited anyone who wanted to know more to call his office, which people did every now and then. One might think an open line to the company president would be abused, yet Ken maintains it never was. "The people who called really wanted to discuss spiritual issues. And because my business was God's business, if He wanted me to take fifteen minutes to talk to someone, that's what I did.

"Believers should not be afraid to be public about their faith," Ken says. "Yes, I've taken flak for being so open about what I believe. However, I've also had people who have given me a bad time come back privately and say they respect the fact that I'm not ashamed of my faith."

Watch out that spiritual boldness doesn't create resentment toward the gospel.

Many Christians would not be comfortable with Eldred's frankness, especially in light of his privileged position at the top. Harvard Business School professor Laura Nash asked Christian executives what level of witnessing they thought was appropriate in the office:

> When does Christian commitment from the chief executive constitute an unfair use of space, and when is it a duty not to be denied simply because the business culture frowns on it? All the interviewees felt that they bore witness in some way in their working life, but the ways in which they deliberately affected the business culture fell into three categories of responses:
> - Overt, institutionalized witnessing through the use of the language, rituals, and symbols of Christianity.
> - Overt but personalized witnessing.
> - Indirect or passive witnessing.[1]

Ken's response to Nash is, "All of the above, and in that order." And he has been effective because of his integrity, consistency, love for people, and love of Christ. Such boldness is not without pitfalls, and Ken is candid about some of his mistakes. "At one stage in my life, I shared my faith very aggressively at work. I would often talk to people who were busy or in a hurry. Some of them got upset because they had things to do. I had to learn to be more sensitive to their time. If they were interested in spiritual things, I needed to set up a lunch or other time to meet so as not to interrupt the business day.

"I had a similar issue with a Bible study I used to conduct during lunch hour. I was not always sensitive to when people needed to be back at their desks. 'I'm late,' some would say, 'but I was with the president.' Their supervisors got mad because I was messing up the work schedules. Finally I put someone else in charge of the study and backed away. It faded and disappeared after that."

While Eldred's vigorous Christianity caused some occasional friction, he never had employees claim they were treated unfairly because of their spiritual views. "Everyone could see that promotions were based on a person's work, not their beliefs," says Ken. "I once asked a fellow executive, who wasn't a Christian, about religious discrimination. He said, 'Don't worry about it, Ken. It's because of you that we have so many nonChristians throughout this organization, including at the highest levels.'"

As Inmac grew, Ken faced the dilemma of every successful entrepreneur, the lessening of his influence over the values initially set in place. "We got to fifteen hundred employees in ten countries," he says, "and it bothered me that I could no longer keep track of the spiritual temperature in the company. I wrestled with how to make sure we were still doing things according to a godly standard. As I was praying about this, God said, 'Look, Ken, I know you have given me your business. If something is not right, I will bring it to your attention. If I do, then I want you to fix the problem. If I don't, don't go looking for trouble.'"

Here's one example of how this arrangement worked. "At one point in our history people were buying software and passing it around the office," Ken relates. "The software companies said, 'Hey, wait a minute! You only have the right to use the software on one computer.' God brought this to my attention and I asked the IT manager if this was going on. He said 'yes.' When I told him it was wrong, he replied, 'Everyone does it.' 'I don't care if everyone does it,' I answered. 'We need to do what's right before God.' This man wasn't a Christian, but he accepted what I said. I asked what it would cost to pay for all the software we used. He came back two weeks later with a figure of $250,000, which we couldn't afford. I told him that God would provide the funds; no more sharing software. Well, the year went by and we made our numbers, in spite of the [money] spent on software. I don't know how God did it, but it worked and we all learned a valuable lesson."

Eldred found other opportune moments to bring up God. One of his favorites was during the hiring process. He would tell prospective hires how important it was for him to know what motivated them as potential employees. After they responded, he would say, "'You need to know what motivates me as an employer in order to understand how I operate and why things happen the way they do around here.' Their motivation didn't have to be the same as mine; it never affected the hiring process. But the discussion gave me a chance to share my faith with people."

Raise awareness of God through public acts of dependence upon Him.

Overt displays of faith such as those mentioned earlier can create sharing opportunities. Praying as part of normal business operations can be another door opener. If done flippantly it can easily backfire, but it can be very powerful if done carefully. Reaching back to Inmac's early days, Eldred tells of the time, "I had four or five employees, and none of them were Christians. Sales were way down and we were very worried. My wife and I had been praying and the Lord showed us that we would have a $7,000 day that Monday instead of our average $2,200. I sat down with my employees and said, 'God has told me we're going to have a $7,000 day.' The look on their faces said, 'I'd better update my resume. This guy has flipped his lid!'

"As the day wore on, our customer rep came into my office to announce that we could actually have a $5,000 day. I said, 'No, Nancy, $7,000 is what we're expecting.' At 5 P.M. we added the total twice and it came to $7,050. The employees were just as excited as I was. Talk about making an impression!"

Prayer is so important to Ken that it permeates his leadership style. It was standard operating procedure at banquets, meetings, and company lunches. If an employee or executive came to him with a difficult personal issue, Ken would offer to pray with them. "I've never had anyone say no," he says. "I've seen men cry who never shed tears before because they were deeply touched by someone caring enough to pray with them."

Inmac merged with Microwarehouse in 1996, and this provided another chance to talk about Jesus. The day of the merger, Eldred told the new chairman, "'You're taking over a company that's been very important to me. I've built it from scratch to around $400 million in revenues. I'm happy for you to have it, but I want to give you something more important.' At that point I shared my faith in Jesus Christ. After thirty minutes he thanked me and went into the then-president's office. 'Eldred just talked to me about Jesus,' he stammered. 'Is he serious?' The president, who is also a Christian, smiled and said, 'Yes he is.'"

Ken left Inmac after the sale and cofounded Ariba Technologies, Inc., an Internet-based B2B platform. He and his wife, Roberta, also started Living Stones Foundation to encourage Christian work around the world. Today the Eldreds remain active in business and spiritual endeavors that span the globe. Their horizons have broadened as their wealth has increased. Still, their foundation remains the same, a commitment to put Christ first in everything. They have proven the reality of Jesus' promise, "But seek first his [God's] kingdom and his righteousness, and all these things will be given to you as well" (Matthew 6:33). They have also taken to heart His warning, "If anyone is ashamed of me and my words, the Son of Man will be ashamed of him when he comes in his glory and in the glory of the Father and of the holy angels" (Luke 9:26).

Given the rewards of commitment and the risks of concealment, Ken thinks the biggest mistake Christians make is remaining quiet about their faith. It's a mistake he's determined not to make.

Other Voices

I once had an employee who I hoped would find Christ, but she wasn't open to the gospel. A speaker came to town for an outreach event and I said to this woman, "I'd like you to be at this dinner party." She took this as an order rather than an invitation. The speaker came on way too strong, telling everyone they had to decide for Christ right NOW! The woman felt very pressured. I was embarrassed and apologized. Later, she left the firm and filed a lawsuit. One of her grievances was my pressure to "change her religion." I've since learned to be more careful.

George Cook, senior vice president, Smith Barney

When I met with potential hires to explain our company's vision and values, I would ask them to tell me a bit about their life's journey and then ask about their spiritual journey. When they finished I would say, "That's great; now I would like to tell you about my journey. Many times this would create further discussion regarding spiritual things. I would generally give the individual a copy of John Stott's *Becoming a Christian* and *Being a Christian*. Speaking of books, we developed an active reading program among our employees. Some selections were Christian books that usually stimulated good discussion.

Bob Fulton, former CEO of Web Industries

Your Turn

Find a context in which you can give your testimony—at church, at the Rotary Club, at a prayer breakfast. Have it professionally taped and transcribed. Then look for opportunities to pass it on to anyone who wants to know more about you than what's on your business card. The apostle Paul often recounted his experience of God's grace as a way to "gossip" the gospel.

Chapter Five
Custom Fit

One of the apostle Paul's favorite metaphors for believers is the body of Christ. "Just as each of us has one body with many members, and these members do not all have the same function," he wrote, "so in Christ we who are many form one body, and each member belongs to all the others. We have different gifts, according to the grace given us" (Romans 12:4-6).

What is true of spiritual gifts is also true of natural temperaments and personal callings. The extroverted apostle who wrote these words differed from the introverted Timothy, who became his most valued disciple. Peter, "the Rock," was not at all like John, "the disciple whom Jesus loved." Lydia, the entrepreneur who helped start the church in Philippi, had a dissimilar temperament from Priscilla, the mentor of Apollos.

This diversity among disciples is by design. Today it would be hard to find two more dedicated Christian executives with more diverse approaches to their callings than Ken Eldred (chapter 4) and Dale Gifford. Eldred started his own company and preached and prayed there openly. Gifford took the helm of Hewitt Associates after twenty years of working his way to the top, and maintains a more quiet testimony. Ken has the disposition of an evangelist; Dale, that of an actuary. (Dale chuckles at the joke that an actuary is someone who finds accounting too exciting.) Both men have earned the respect of their peers because of their business acumen, and the right to be heard because of their personal integrity. How they exercise that right is a study in contrasts.

Testify according to your temperament; play to your strengths.

Hewitt Associates is a billion-dollar management consulting and outsourcing firm that specializes in human resource solutions. It's the largest benefits consulting business in the U.S. and the second largest on the planet. The company was included in the initial lists of the 100 Best Companies to Work for in America, in the late 1980s and early 1990s. Since then, Hewitt has been asked to help in the annual selections (now in *Fortune* magazine), which disqualifies them from further inclusion.

At the head of this "Best" company is a good man. Dale Gifford, who became chief executive in 1992, is the product of a small Wisconsin town. He joined the firm in 1972 as an actuary after graduating with honors from the University of Wisconsin. The company had about 140 associates (they don't have employees) at the time. Today they have nearly thirteen thousand working in thirty-seven countries.

Dale is not the preachy sort, but those who work with him know the central role faith plays in his leadership style. "We don't pray at board meetings," Gifford says matter-of-factly. "I don't regularly have a Bible on my desk, and I have not written anything specific about my faith to the whole organization. However, I've been around more than thirty years in a number of positions and people know I'm a Christian. I've attended church with quite a few Hewitt folks and been in Bible studies with many of them."

People talk. The word spreads, and Dale says, "I regularly get e-mail from associates I've never met who write, 'I know you are a Christian, and I'd like to thank you for the position you took on this or that issue.' I have had partners ask me if I would come and talk to the leadership at their churches. But while my faith is no secret, I am very careful not to use my authority to intimidate people or cause those of other faiths to feel their opportunities are limited because they hold different religious views."

Gifford pauses for a moment before mentioning some executives he knows who take a more "in your face" approach to Christianity. "This aggressiveness creates concerns among subordinates as to whether their spiritual beliefs, or lack thereof, will limit their careers. As CEO, I have to be very sensitive to this. On one hand I applaud such forthrightness—nobody can spend fifteen minutes with these people without knowing where they stand—yet I believe this detracts from the inclusive environment we strive to maintain. We certainly don't limit our hiring and promoting to Christians or to people we think we can convert."

Dale prefers a more relational style of workplace evangelism, saying, "In the right setting—over dinner, or while traveling—the discussion may get around to questions of faith. At times like that it's very appropriate to speak up. Of course, this assumes the Christian executive is personally accessible and hasn't let position or title get in the way of relationships."

The operative phrase for Christians in executive roles is, "using the position without abusing the power." A leadership position carries a certain level of credibility and visibility. There's always the danger of using this platform as a power base from which to intimidate others into a certain way of thinking. Christians must avoid this trap.

Remember that credibility comes from your words matching your character and actions.

No one likes to be manipulated or exploited by higher-ups. But when supervisors earn one's respect by their character or how they do their jobs, subordinates are more open to, and less threatened by, their influence. "The credibility I've gained by how I perform gives me opportunities at work, in the community, and even in the church," Gifford says. "However, there's a flip side to this higher profile. Christian executives must realize that people are constantly watching us, looking for inconsistencies between what we say and do. It always saddens me when I see a brother or sister stumble. It happens all too often in business and in politics. I think leaders are more vulnerable to personal and moral failure than others. That's one reason I'm involved with a group called Leadership Catalyst. They stress the importance of character development keeping pace with skill development."

Catalyst president, Bruce McNicol, warns that,

> Success, as defined by our culture, tends to breed loneliness and personal failure in leaders. It seems the higher leaders climb, the more isolated and separated they become from their employees, friends, spouses and children. Leaders ultimately experience a deep sense of loneliness amidst their success. We want to change this by altering the prevailing definition of success to one that includes healthy character development amidst authentic relationships of trust within an environment of grace.[1]

Speaking of environments, Gifford's consistency through the years has been helped by the fact that Hewitt, while not a "Christian" company, has been an ethical one. The values and the integrity with which they operate are consistent with the teachings of Christianity. "As long as I have been involved with this organization," Gifford affirms, "I've never been asked to do anything that would compromise my faith. This is attributable to our founder, Ted Hewitt, and the kind of people he hired. The positive atmosphere he created is something we strive to help our clients create as well. A key to this is the compelling and profound notion that organizations can have win-win relationships with their people. Every individual in the organizations where we work or consult is important to us. This valuation fits strongly with the Christian message of the dignity of human beings as created in God's image."

This concept will be familiar to Stephen Covey readers. Habit Four of his famous *Seven Habits of Highly Effective People* is, "Think win-win," which he defines as, "a frame of mind and heart that constantly seeks mutual benefit in all human interactions. . . .Win-win is based on the paradigm that there is plenty for everybody, that one person's success is not achieved at the expense or exclusion of the success of others."[2]

Business consultant Rolf Osterberg notes the benefits of this more holistic and healthy way of treating people:

> I'm not saying a company should not be profitable, but a company will grow when those working there grow as human beings. Profit and eventual expansion are by-products of the process. We have developed into a production-oriented society. And to make the economic system spin, we have to consume everything we produce. Can what we call economic growth, ever-increasing production and consumption, really be meaningful anymore?

Real growth is more than increasing production and con-
sumption. Real growth is not [just] economic growth. It
is personal/human growth.[3]

Look for a position that utilizes your natural talents and spiritual gifts.

Gifford's own journey of personal growth and spiritual maturity has
been a gradual one. He attended church as a kid, but didn't have a relationship with God. After college and marriage, he and his wife, Becky,
got involved in a church they found through the yellow pages. They
chose a nondenominational congregation so they wouldn't have to
decide between his Methodist background and her Church of Christ
background. Over the next few years Becky became a committed Christian. Through her example and the consistent sharing of a few men Dale
greatly respected, he came to a personal relationship with Christ in his
mid-twenties.

"In many ways it was an intellectual journey with a significant step
of faith at the end," Gifford says. "I had to work through lots of questions
to get to where I could take that leap. Along the way I learned that I didn't
have to suspend my intellectual faculties in order to believe. I also came
to understand that a holy God doesn't grade on a curve. Simply being less
evil than most people isn't enough. We all fall short of God's expectations
and need to be personally forgiven for our sins. The perfect sacrifice of
Jesus Christ is the only way to bridge the gap between God and man."

As Gifford got to know his Bible, he discovered that when the
Holy Spirit places Christians into the body of Christ at conversion, He
also equips them with gifts for ministry. Often these gifts parallel or aug-
ment natural talents. The combination thereof prepares believers for effective service in their chosen vocations.

Gifford feels strongly that God has equipped and called him to the top position at Hewitt for a reason. "My life today is a process of discovering what the Lord wants me to do in this role. My CEO position doesn't make me a better person than someone with a different calling. Paul says in Romans 12, 'Do not think of yourself more highly than you ought, but rather think of yourself with sober judgment, in accordance with the measure of faith God has given you.' It's vital to maintain an appropriate sense of humility, a sort of separation between who you are and what you do. I have seen this powerfully modeled by top executives like Bill Pollard at ServiceMaster and Don Soderquist, former COO at Wal-Mart.

"Bob Buford's catch phrase, 'moving beyond success to significance,' has greatly influenced my thinking," Gifford adds, "especially when it comes to the imprint I leave on this organization, our people, and our clients around the world. It also relates to how I use my money and other forms of influence for which I will be held accountable. I have been given such tremendous opportunities and I want to be careful not to underutilize them."

Spiritual gifts and leadership opportunities are given to Christians for one reason—service. "You know that those who are regarded as rulers of the Gentiles lord it over them," Jesus once told the disciples, "and their high officials exercise authority over them. Not so with you. Instead, whoever wants to become great among you must be your servant, and whoever wants to be first must be slave of all. For even the Son of Man did not come to be served, but to serve, and to give his life as a ransom for many" (Mark 10:41-45).

We can serve most effectively in the position that fits our unique calling and giftedness, no matter where that puts us on the organizational chart. This will be our personal "best place" to influence others. It will also be the perfect spot from which to impress the One we long to hear say, "Well done, good and faithful servant!"

Other Voices

Talk of retirement is common these days at my company. I've studied our plan over the years and am referred to as the local expert. Every week at least one associate will ask me to explain something. I try to answer their questions and then mention that besides the money for retirement, they'll need their health to really enjoy it. They ponder that, we talk some more, then I often ask, "What about after retirement? What about eternity?" That question has led to some great discussions and even a personal commitment or two. I've done this for more than ten years and have only had one person ask not to continue the conversation.

Dan Tadie, control systems supervisor,
Colorado Springs Utilities

Several years ago I led a lunchtime Bible study that was not given permission to meet on-site. Rather than make an issue, we met at a neutral location. This planned activity was good, but I've found the most important thing—and usually the hardest—is to be continually available to minister in small ways to subordinates or supervisors. My most fruitful opportunities have come on the spur of the moment. The challenge is to be ready for these divine appointments.

Gary Rapp, former asset development manager,
Amerada Hess Corporation

Your Turn

Provide for the whole person as part of your company's health care plan. Hire a full- or part-time chaplain. Or, ask a local pastor to visit regularly as a volunteer chaplain. Underwrite the services of a Christian counseling agency to offer free or discounted help to those who are open to God's answers to life's problems. For chaplain information, contact Marketplace Ministries at 800-775-7657 or visit their web site at www.marketplaceministries.com.

Chapter Six

Owner's Privilege

While there is no such thing as a "Christian" company, there are Christians who start companies in answer to a sense of calling. These believer-entrepreneurs are after something more valuable than money or the freedom of self-determination. They are compelled to turn their dreams into reality and are willing, in the words of the Garth Brooks' country song, to "choose to chance the rapids (and) dare to dance the tides" rather than "sit upon the shoreline."[1]

Few entrepreneurs succeed. Most who launch into the currents of modern commerce go under, as best-selling author and business guru Michael Gerber points out:

> Businesses start and fail in the United States at an increasingly staggering rate. Every year, over a million people in this country start a business of some sort. Statistics tell us that by the end of the first year at least 40 percent of them will be out of business. Within five years, more than 80 percent of them—800,000—will have failed. And

the rest of the bad news is, if you own a small business that has managed to survive for five years or more, don't breathe a sigh of relief. Because more than 80 percent of the small businesses that survive the first five years fail in the second five.[2]

If entrepreneurs manage to keep their crafts afloat, they earn the right to be the captains of their ships. They get to set the course and say how things will be done on board. This includes determining the profile they will give to personal faith.

Be open about your faith without being overbearing.

Ray Berryman is a passionate believer who is active in his local church and several Christian organizations. His spiritual ardor carries over into his professional life, where he is chairman of the board and CEO of Berryman & Henigar Enterprises, a civil engineering business he started in 1975 that now has annual revenues north of $40 million. From the start, gospel tracts have been conspicuous in the lobby at corporate headquarters. Ray's favorites are *The Four Spiritual Laws* and *Got Life?* Josh McDowell's *More Than a Carpenter* and Billy Graham's materials are also free for the taking. He encourages employee-initiated prayer meetings and Bible studies at the office, although he doesn't lead these himself. Every year at the Christmas party he shares a clear gospel message and invites everyone to accept the gift of salvation.

"People know I'm a Christian, and that's good," Ray says. "Potential hires will often mention that the reason they want to join our firm is because they've heard we practice Christian principles. Many executives have Bibles on their desks. We give ten percent of our pre-tax profits to Christian ministries. We open our business meetings with prayer. If someone protests any of these practices, I simply, lovingly, explain that we have the right to do this."

Berryman makes a distinction between being open and being overbearing. He doesn't usually initiate evangelistic conversations and is careful not to intimidate employees or visitors. Spiritual conversations are normally postponed until after work. "People can usually wait till then," he says. "However, if I perceive someone is truly seeking, I will talk to them on business time. As the apostle Peter says, 'But in your hearts set apart Christ as Lord. Always be prepared to give an answer to everyone who asks you to give the reason for the hope that you have'(1 Peter 3:15). And as for prayer, if a trauma happens in a person's life such as an injury or the loss of a loved one, I offer to pray for them on the spot. This may open a door to share my faith later, especially if they receive comfort through those prayers. I don't do this as an evangelistic maneuver. I believe deeply in the power of prayer and feel it is the most compassionate thing I can do for people in times of need."

Having said all this, Berryman hastens to add that he certainly doesn't require faith as a condition for employment or advancement. Promotions are based on performance, not on personal beliefs. He thinks CEOs and other executives should avoid fueling internal politics with their own prejudices. And Christianity can be seen as one such prejudice.

Respond graciously but firmly to those who oppose legitimate expressions of faith.

On a few occasions, nonChristian employees have been offended by Berryman's public displays of faith. "I had a Muslim working for me in a very senior position," Ray remembers. "One Christmas I gave everyone a Jesus video and this bothered him. He mentioned that he had enjoyed our Christmas parties, but for years he had been offended by the gospel message I gave. He worked under a senior vice president who was also a Muslim, and when that VP left to start his own company, this gentleman went with him. Two years later he called to say he wanted to come back because he knew that we stood on good moral principles. I rehired him and today he's one of our highest performers. I find it interesting that he would choose to work in a Christian environment rather than a Muslim one.

"Another time I got in trouble because of my practice of giving New Testaments to my employees. I received an angry letter from a Jewish man who was very upset by this. His attack hurt my feelings, but I decided to accept it as part of being a witness, as 2 Timothy 3:12 says: 'Everyone who wants to live a godly life in Christ Jesus will be persecuted.'"

A witness is somebody who sees or hears something that has happened and gives testimony about it. When Jesus called Saul of Tarsus to become Paul the apostle, He said, "I have appeared to you to appoint you as a servant and as a witness of what you have seen of me and what I will show you" (Acts 26:16). The privilege of testifying carries with it the prerequisite of forethought, as Harvard Business School Professor Laura Nash notes:

> A key feature of being a witness is the willingness to explain how one's faith works and to share personal experiences. Being prepared is important. Asserted former Secretary of State Jim Baker at the 1991 National Prayer Breakfast: "I really do believe that those of us who are put in positions of public trust really shouldn't be hesitant to speak about spiritual values. In fact, I happen to believe that spiritual values are important in the pursuit of world peace."[3]

Berryman's advice to other Christian business owners is straightforward. "Be open about your belief in God. Don't be intimidated or hesitant to express your faith in ways like opening a meeting in prayer when this is appropriate. Just be consistent. Our practices need to be in agreement with the principles we say we believe. This means being open to anybody who sees something that's not in line with our profession. Public faith invites public scrutiny."

Ray's zeal stems from the impact Jesus Christ has had on his own life. "After college I got involved in a strong anticommunist group," he reminisces. "I came from a very conservative free-enterprise background. The more I thought about the West losing out to communism, the more desperate I became. One day I attended a rally where the speaker said that only one force could defeat communism—and all the other evils in the world—and that was Jesus Christ. He told us how we could have joy and peace through a personal relationship with Christ. He made it so simple, and I accepted Jesus as my Savior."

Since then, both Christianity and capitalism have shaped Ray's life. The business he started does not attempt to separate the two. However, Berryman & Henigar Enterprises is a company, not a church. Christian CEOs can integrate faith into corporate culture, and midlevel managers can do the same, but neither should try to convert their companies or departments into churches.

Secular executives have an evangelistic advantage precisely because they are not in church and they are not pastors, as Will Perkins, chairman of Perkins Motor City Dodge, points out:

> As a salesman, I know the strongest recommendation
> for a product comes from a satisfied customer. If I'm at
> a gas station and someone asks about the new car I'm
> driving, I can give him lots of information. But if he finds

out I'm a car salesman, he will probably say, "Oh," and drive off. However, if I were not a salesman and I said, "This is the best car I've ever owned," the guy would most likely want to know more. When a preacher talks about God, people aren't impressed because that's his job. I've had hundreds of opportunities to share the gospel with people who observe my life because I'm not a preacher, but a salesman who loves to talk about my relationship with Jesus Christ.

Know what's acceptable and unacceptable on the job and don't cross the line.

Even if you are the company founder and CEO, there are legal issues to consider when discussing God at work. William Diehl, president of Riverbend Resource Center, offers the following list of "unofficial rules" from an article in the *Los Angeles Times*:

- It is acceptable to keep a copy of the Bible or the Koran on one's desk.
- One may ask a coworker if he or she has "found Jesus Christ," but one may not stuff tracts into a coworker's in-box, desk drawer, or work files.
- It is acceptable for employees to meet in an empty conference room for a lunchtime prayer session, but a supervisor cannot schedule an important meeting that "just happens" to be preceded by a Christian prayer session.
- It is acceptable to wear a yarmulke, crucifix, or Star of David to work, but one may not chant in such a way as to distract other workers.

- It is acceptable to talk around the water cooler about religion, but planned corporate religious retreats are taboo.
- It is acceptable for a supervisor to invite employees to a son's bar mitzvah, but a supervisor may not question an employee about his or her lack of church attendance last Sunday.[4]

Christian owners or executives don't have to hide their faith, but they can't force it on their people either. Even well-meaning practices like praying for employees can be misinterpreted. "Be careful," cautions management consultant John Bradley. "I know a business owner who is very open about his faith and who takes time to pray for anyone who comes to him. While he is a respected person, this approach has created a two-class system in his company. Some of his employees view prayer as a political tool used to butter up the boss and they resent it."

The best way to discern what's appropriate on the job is a moment-by-moment sensitivity to the Holy Spirit. Executives can often visualize board members scrutinizing and influencing their actions; why not the Holy Spirit? "I try to keep this perspective at all times," says Berryman. "It helps me focus on the task at hand, which is honoring Jesus Christ in everything."

Honoring God can lead to blessings, both spiritual and financial. Engineering News-Record ranks Berryman & Henigar among the top two hundred and fifty engineering consulting companies. This has opened doors in the U.S. and abroad. "I recently went to Ecuador to talk with various leaders about 'True Success and How to Change the World,'" Berryman reports. "You don't get invited to talk with these kind of people unless you have something they want. My company has not only given me a way to make a good living, but it provides a platform from which I can present the gospel."

From a biblical perspective, work is meant to be about more than earning a living. It's an expression of who we are and what we value. It's more than a job; it's how we reflect the image of a creative Creator. For some, their work is to provide meaningful employment for others. Such entrepreneurs become owners and their companies become places where people can find and fulfill their vocations.

Now, if a company is an expression of an entrepreneur's faith in God, why shouldn't that faith be visible? And if Christian business owners care deeply about their people, how can those owners not share the love of God with them?

"This is good," says the apostle Paul, "and pleases God our Savior, who wants all men to be saved and to come to a knowledge of the truth. For there is one God and one mediator between God and men, the man Christ Jesus, who gave himself as a ransom for all men—the testimony given in its proper time" (1 Timothy 2:3-6).

Herein lies the balance for which Christians must constantly strive: giving the testimony of God's love—at the proper time.

Other Voices

Friends, customers, and employees always notice plaques and awards. On my walls I had autographed pictures of Billy Graham and other religious figures, along with awards from some of the Christian organizations I have supported. These were great conversation-starters about faith.

W. Robert Stover, chairman of Westaff

When it comes to organizing religious events, be sure you know your company's rules as to how far you can go on company time or property. As an executive, can you lead a Bible study? Can you be a guest at an employee-organized study? What about times of prayer?

And when you do participate in such activities, always display a "kingdom view" of Christianity. Don't emphasize denominational nuances or doctrinal differences.

Daniel Dominguez, partner of BDO Seidman, LLP

YOUR TURN

Whenever you are invited to speak to a person or group because of your business expertise, work in a reference to your "life-changing experience" without saying directly what it is. Be prepared to follow up with your testimony with anyone who asks for more details. Give the inquirer a booklet such as *The Four Spiritual Laws* or *Bridge to Life* to help the person visualize the steps to salvation.

Chapter Seven
Celebrating Diversity

Americans tend to gather in homogeneous groups and this goes for our churches. This comfortable segregation goes counter to the message and model of Jesus Christ. His initial disciples included sinful women, political extremists, half-breed Samaritans, outcast lepers, Roman centurions, Gentile demoniacs, and respected rabbis. After His resurrection, He sent His followers to the four corners of the earth with the good news that all peoples are invited to the great feast (see Acts 1:8; Luke 14:15-23).

As lifelong Jews, the apostles needed some extra persuasion to break out of their ethnic mind-set (see Acts 10 and 11). Paul got the point right away and taught, "You are all sons of God through faith in Christ Jesus, for all of you who were baptized into Christ have clothed yourselves with Christ. There is neither Jew nor Greek, slave nor free, male nor female, for you are all one in Christ Jesus" (Galatians 3:26-28).

Reaching out and accepting those who are "different" demonstrates the life-changing power of the gospel, with Paul himself being Exhibit A. One modern disciple who agrees with the old apostle's appreciation for diversity is Donna Auguste, founder of Freshwater Software and the Leave a Little Room Foundation (LLR). "As an African-American woman, I'm used to being in the minority," Donna says. "I'm very comfortable with that. I'm also very passionate about diversity. As a leader, I make it a point to be inclusive, which means respecting the different beliefs and flavors that are part of the mix."

Display the gospel's inclusiveness by reaching across natural barriers.

The fabric of Donna's life has always been varied. "I grew up in Berkeley, California immersed in a community of diversity," she recalls. "In Catholic grade school I received a solid academic and spiritual foundation. I began learning to listen to God and follow His directions. Then I switched to public high school and got into a special engineering and science program. I studied engineering at UC Berkeley and went on to Carnegie-Mellon's graduate program in computer science."

After graduation, life went from fast to faster. Donna joined a start-up company that pioneered commercial artificial intelligence software. A few years later she became the software project manager for Apple's Newton, the world's first Personal Digital Assistant. She then moved to Boulder, Colorado, where she became senior director at US West and led an engineering team that developed a fiber-optic broadband network.

In 1996, Auguste and a colleague, John Meier, left US West to start Freshwater Software, a company that now supplies web monitoring solutions to e-commerce-centric organizations. The firm did very well and was acquired by Mercury Interactive in 2001. "At Freshwater, we had an opportunity to start a company from scratch and to shape its culture," says Donna. "Even before John and I had a name for the business, or knew what our product would be, we decided to focus on customer service and cultural diversity. As John likes to joke, we had diversity when there were just the two of us.

"When I say, 'go deep with diversity,' I mean all kinds of diversity: ethnic, gender, age, education, social beliefs, everything. Just look at the life of Jesus. What a wonderful example of working with people from diverse backgrounds and situations. Christianity was born because of how He reached out to all kinds of folks without requiring them to change first."

Embracing diversity doesn't mean that truth is subjective, or that all roads lead to the same place. But it does mean respecting people for who they are, and relating to them where they are. Christians should be like thoughtful travelers who have found a reliable guide for life's arduous journey. The stereotypical Ugly American has been defined as a boorish, nationalistic American, traveling abroad, who gives Americans a bad reputation. The Ugly Christian is an egotistical, self-absorbed citizen of heaven, traveling abroad, who gives Christ a bad name.

When Jesus walked on earth, He was accessible to everyone from priests to prostitutes. A person couldn't stay in His presence for long without changing or leaving, but all were welcome to get as close as they wanted. We should aspire to be as winsome and open as Jesus, and as forthcoming with the truth when the time is right.

Find provocative things to do that will stimulate spiritual conversations.

Creating an atmosphere of acceptance doesn't mean fusing everything into a dull gray sameness. Blending shouldn't lead to blandness but to rich flavor. Executives who encourage others to "be themselves" will be able to express their own selves most freely. Without abusing her executive position, Donna looks for some small thing to do that might lead to a spiritual conversation. "I try to show others what I've learned from Jesus by the way I live," she explains. "Actions speak much louder than words, and I've found that even small actions can open up opportunities to talk about my faith."

Too much salt will irritate and burn. That's why Christians in places of authority need to be careful not to pour it on when they talk about their faith. However, a little salt in the right place can create a thirst for the Water of Life. Here are a few instances from Donna's career that show how a little seasoning goes a long way.

"One time the systems administrator at a company I worked for was helping me fix an e-mail problem. When he asked for my password, I told him it was 'Deuteronomy 6.' 'I don't even know how to spell that!' he said. 'What is it?' I told him it was an important chapter in the Bible and I opened the Bible I had on my desk. I handed it to him and he sat there and read it. This is exactly what I love to do: create curiosity and respond to people's questions.

"I gave away a lot of Bibles," Donna adds, "but generally not to employees in a work situation. I always made sure there were Bibles around, and if somebody picked one up and took it home, that was great. I also invited people to my church and many of them came. Sometimes it helped them find what they were looking for; sometimes it didn't."

Prayer is another way Donna raises the issue of God at work. "I never opened corporate meetings with prayer, but whenever someone asked me how I handled tough business situations, I always told them that I prayed. That's where I get my answers. Sometimes I'm talking to God all day long."

Professor and author Dallas Willard defines prayer as "a conversation with God about what we are doing together," and says the dynamic behind it is "the power of asking continued over time." It is different from, and more useful than worry, in that worry is talking to yourself while prayer is talking to Someone who can do something about your situation.

Finally, Donna is very open about her role models. She recalls, "One time a journalist who was interviewing me asked if I had a mentor and I replied, 'Yes, Jesus Christ.' He was not happy with this and countered, 'No, no, I meant somebody who's living,' and I fired back, 'He is living. That's the whole point!'"

The philosopher-priest Henri Nouwen once wrote:

> The task of future Christian leaders is not to make a little contribution to the solution of the pains and tribulations of their time, but to identify and announce the ways in which Jesus is leading God's people out of slavery, through the desert to a new land of freedom. Christian leaders have the arduous task of responding to personal struggles, family conflicts, national calamities, and international tensions [not to mention business crises] with an articulate faith in God's real presence.[1]

Such leadership needs to be modeled in the workplace, not just in churches and religious organizations.

When it comes to leading a small team, or a whole company, executives often have a vision for what it means to be successful. Donna believes that Christians sometimes shrink their goals because they think it's wrong to aim too high. "The challenge for Christians in leadership is to remember that our God is an awesome God," she insists. "He does things like create the universe. And sometimes our awesome God chooses to have us do amazing work. That can be intimidating and make us want to run away and hide, or aim for something smaller."

The opposing danger is aiming high, hitting your target, and then taking the credit. "It's right there in Deuteronomy 8," warns Auguste. "We are told not to forget where we come from; not to forget the God who has brought us through the desert and has blessed us. It is not by our power or brilliance that we get anything done. I've seen the limitations of my own knowledge and resources. I'm incredibly limited, but God is not. If we're hooked up with Him, we can achieve anything He wants us to. We can accomplish whatever He has in mind, and He has a pretty wild imagination."

Blend prayer and action to produce results that reveal God's presence.

So how can Christians discern between their own grandiose plans and the Lord's vision? "First, listen to God and follow His leading," Donna suggests. "I talk to God all the time. I listen to Him. I let Him direct my life as much as I can. I'm very passionate about what I do because I know it's all the Lord's work. Whether I'm playing my bass guitar at church, being CEO of Freshwater, starting a foundation like Leave a Little Room, or teaching computer classes to seniors at the community center, it's all for Him. Second, follow the example of Nehemiah. The book he wrote is one of the most inspiring to me as a businessperson. I read it over and over again. Nehemiah had a wonderful blend of prayer and action so needed by leaders and executives. Through prayer, we lock our eyes onto the right goals. Action is the follow-through, getting it done.

"That's not all," says Donna. "Nehemiah was very resourceful in completing a task that had been left unfinished for over seventy years. He outlined what needed to be done; he united the people around the vision; he overcame obstacles; and through it all the pattern is the same. He paused to pray, and then decided to do 'X.' This created some problems, so he stopped to pray and then moved ahead and did 'Y.' When a new crisis arose, he prayed once more, and then did 'Z.' Prayer and action were like his two legs; he used them together to keep moving forward."

Chuck Swindoll also appreciates this concert of prayer and performance. The need for leaders to act is obvious, but why is prayer so important?

> Here are the four shortest reasons I know: Prayer makes
> me wait. I cannot pray and work at the same time. I have
> to wait to act until I finish praying. Prayer forces me to
> leave the situation with God; it makes me wait. Secondly,
> prayer clears my vision. . . . When you first face a situa-
> tion, is it foggy? Prayer will "burn through." Your vision will
> clear so you can see through God's eyes. Thirdly, prayer
> quiets my heart. . . . It replaces anxiety with a calm spirit.
> Knees don't knock when we kneel on them! Fourthly,
> prayer activates my faith. After praying I am more prone
> to trust God.[2]

"I've tried to behave the same in every situation," Donna maintains, "whether as part of a team at Apple, or running my own company, or being active in my church. Part of my calling is to be out there among people, listening, learning, and participating in a hands-on way. Much of what I'm doing these days flows through the foundation I started before selling Freshwater. I created an endowment for Leave a Little Room that will allow us to expand what we're doing and to launch our Gospel Music Initiative. This is a global effort to bring together different sources of spiritual music and to share that music around the world. We also sponsor a variety of other projects like developing solar-electrical systems for schools and clinics in Tanzania."

Despite appearances, Donna's activism doesn't come naturally. "I'm an introverted person," she says, "yet most of the things God has called me to do are extroverted tasks. For the most part I don't wonder why; I just enjoy the opportunities. Every now and then I get off track, but I try to make sure that I am doing God's will with the talents and resources He's put into my care."

"And whatever you do," admonished Paul, "whether in word or deed, do it all in the name of the Lord Jesus, giving thanks to God the Father through him" (Colossians 3:17). There is a lot of "whatever" in most of our lives, and we should be tackling it with relish.

Or should we say, with salt?

Other Voices

As the commander of a military processing station, it was my responsibility to welcome the new recruits and give them some words of wisdom for the day. Since the previous commander had been a believer, I was able to continue the tradition of handing out thousands of green Gideon New Testaments. Each day I told the recruits of the difficult journey ahead and recommended they use the Green Book as a resource. It was remarkable how many men and women wrote back thanking us for the "ultimate training manual."

Phil Carman, USAF (retired)

When I was a junior member of a larger company, I organized a regular Bible study. However, when I became a CEO, I did not start a study because I thought it would create an "in-group" and cause ill will among those who did not attend. I don't use my position as CEO as a vehicle to speak into someone's life without being invited to do so. I pray that people will recognize a connection between my behavior and my faith. When they ask about the source of my behavior, I invite them to a non-work setting to hear the reasons for my behavior—the gospel of Jesus Christ.

Larry Donnithorne, author of *The West Point Way of Leadership*

YOUR TURN

Research upcoming events with a spiritual component that might be appropriate ("safe") to invite employees or associates to attend. Groups like CBMC (Christian Business Men's Committee) at 800-566-2262, and Executive Ministries at 864-370-3115, sponsor such activities. Prayer breakfasts, executive luncheons, and golf tournaments are all venues where people can be exposed to the gospel in nonthreatening ways.

Chapter Eight

Rights and Responsibilities

D
r. M. F. Bradford of the University of Dallas once pointed out that at least fifty of the fifty-six men who signed the Declaration of Independence were members in good standing of local churches. Of the fifty-five signers of the U. S. Constitution, he found that at least fifty were professing, orthodox Christians.[1] The Constitution forbids the American government to institute, or interfere with, the practice of religion or the expression thereof. When that government puts forth social policies that impinge on our ability to determine our own moral behavior, Christians have the right to resist. And when it tries to restrict religious freedom in the workplace, Christian executives have a responsibility to exercise their constitutional rights.

"Everyone must submit himself to the governing authorities," commands the apostle Paul, "for there is no authority except that which God has established" (Romans 13:1). In America, the government derives its authority from the Constitution, not from a particular administration or session of Congress. This means it's possible for believers to affirm the former while resisting the latter when it contradicts the Constitution. One Christian executive who has been in this predicament is

John Beckett. He's the chairman and CEO of The R. W. Beckett Corporation, a worldwide leader in the manufacture and sales of heating components. Its various companies have over five hundred employees and annual sales approaching $100 million. John had no idea his father's sudden death in 1965 would start him on the road to becoming a renowned industry leader and a powerful voice against federal intrusion into the private sector.

Take a public stand when necessary to keep government policies from eroding religious freedoms.

"Private companies aren't exempt from social and legal pressures," Beckett warns. "As legislation moves toward more social engineering we have to be vigilant so that religious—and other—freedoms are not eroded by government policy." He knows the danger firsthand, having tangled with the EEOC (Equal Employment Opportunity Commission) over proposed guidelines that would have severely restricted religious freedom in the workplace. Notices on bulletin boards, discussions about spiritual issues, even a Bible on an employee's desk—anything that could have given the perception of religious discrimination—were in jeopardy.

"It comes down to the question of what constitutes harassment," John explains. "A broad definition could be used as a wedge to introduce various kinds of social reengineering. There are those in government and the public sector who would like to see this happen. Current laws and the EEOC guidelines based on the 1964 Civil Rights Act provide for a considerable amount of religious freedom. It is important this not be abridged."

Besides curtailing expressions of personal faith, the government has also attempted to dictate policy on moral issues. Companies have been pressured to provide benefits for same sex partners, for example. That's a dilemma, especially for Christians. Beckett cites an issue he almost had to face at the beginning of the Clinton administration. "They wanted us to include abortions in our medical coverage. That was on the health-care agenda being pushed at the time. Fortunately it got derailed, but it could come up again."

Beckett and most believers who get drawn into the political process aren't trying to force their morality on others. They simply don't want to give up their constitutional right, nor their moral mandate, to live their lives and run their businesses in accordance with their faith. Such a religiously motivated ethic makes many people uncomfortable. "The fear of religion in the public arena is all too typical of Americans, and particularly the intellectual class, today," says former Solicitor General and U.S. Court of Appeals Judge Robert Bork. "Religious conservatives cannot impose their ideas on society except by the usual democratic methods of trying to build majorities and passing legislation. In that they are no different from any other group of people with ideas of what morality requires."[2]

As important as what Christians stand for is how they stand for it, insists award-winning author Philip Yancey:

> The issues facing society are pivotal, and perhaps a culture war is inevitable. But Christians should use different weapons in fighting wars, the "weapons of mercy" in Dorothy Day's wonderful phrase. Jesus declared that we should have one distinguishing mark: not political correctness or moral superiority but love. Paul added that without love nothing we do—no miracle of faith, no theological brilliance, no flaming personal sacrifice—will avail (1 Corinthians 13).[3]

Practical love for our neighbors—Christian and nonChristian alike—is what Jesus had in mind when He told us to be salt and light in the world. We should do all we can to exert a healthy, wholesome influence on society.

Take practical steps to help the disadvantaged in Jesus' name.

Long before raising issues with the EEOC—and years before President George W. Bush started drawing attention to faith-based initiatives—Beckett had been spreading the aroma of Christ through his own faith-based enterprise. "During a time of high unemployment in our area, we set up Advent Industries as a separate manufacturing company to hire and train disadvantaged people, including parolees and drug offenders. Our criteria for hiring was simply, Is this person bad enough? Ed Seabold, a good businessman with a great heart for people, ran the company. Over a twenty-year period, about twelve hundred men and women went through its program. Many washed out, unable to handle the disciplined work environment, but most have gone on to success in other local businesses. Because of their time at Advent, they possessed not only the needed skills, but also a sense of self-worth and purpose. And, most importantly, large numbers came to a vital, personal knowledge of Christ while in the program."

Such practical concern for the less fortunate doesn't always turn out as well. Darrell Schoenig, founder of Ultimate Support Systems, Inc., shares the flip side of hiring the unemployable:

> I ran into a fellow on the street who lived under a bridge.
> After visiting with him for an hour, I offered him a job. It
> never occurred to me to get a buy-in from his soon-to-be

Executive Influence

manager or coworkers; I simply thrust him into the system. Thinking I was being a great witness of Christ's love to my employees, I organized a "shower" for the man, asking them to donate household items, food, and clothing. I rented a small apartment for him, bought him a bicycle, and sat back to watch God work miracles. Within a few weeks my folly became evident. The guy was a hardcore alcoholic, had weak social skills, and frequently went on binges, missing work for days. Resentment among my employees grew by the day over the low productivity, high frustration levels, and shrinking profit-sharing pot. After months of turmoil the guy disappeared. When he reappeared a couple years later I wisely said no to his request for a job.

Christian executives and other believers who have the opportunities, the wherewithal, and the calling to launch companies or nonprofit ministries to help the less fortunate should do so. But such efforts should be extensions of ongoing involvement with people. "If we believe what we say about serving Christ and loving others," Beckett says, "then we are going to be involved in our people's lives. We are going to be visiting the hospitals and the funeral homes, and attending the weddings to which we are invited. I recall visiting a supervisor in the hospital who had worked with me for twenty years. The first words out of his mouth were, 'John, I'm worried.' I thought it was his medical situation, but that wasn't it. He was worried about his spiritual condition. I regrouped and asked him straight out if he wanted to commit his life to Christ. He reached out his large, work-hardened hand to grab mine and said, 'Boy, would I!' It was an amazing experience, made possible by his years of watching, often skeptically, but ultimately getting thirsty for spiritual reality."

This faith encounter happened because John's life gave him credibility in the eyes of his employee—and because John was physically present in the hospital. "At times like these," he says, "Christian executives have to step out of their management roles and be simple servants of Christ. I feel enormously privileged when opportunities to share the Lord present themselves. I never want to be so isolated as a CEO that I can't talk to employees who are having problems."

Many people would feel uncomfortable sharing the gospel at a bedside—or across a dinner table for that matter. "Hospitals have chaplains for these situations," they point out. "Pastors are better equipped to explain Christianity. Besides, what if the person has questions we can't answer? Such discussions are best left to the professionals." We've become so accustomed to the clergy-laity caste system that we forget it didn't exist in the New Testament. It's not that there are no clergy in the church; the reality is that there is no laity, as 1 Peter 2 makes clear: "As you come to him, the living Stone—rejected by men but chosen by God and precious to him— you also, like living stones, are being built into a spiritual house to be a holy priesthood, offering spiritual sacrifices acceptable to God through Jesus Christ. . . . But you are a chosen people, a royal priesthood, a holy nation, a people belonging to God, that you may declare the praises of him who called you out of darkness into his wonderful light" (verses 4-5, 9).

Take pride in serving as Christ's ambassador in the marketplace.

In addition to being "royal priests," declaring the praises of Him who called us out of darkness, Christians are also to be "Christ's ambassadors," imploring others to be reconciled to God (2 Corinthians 5:20).

A few ambassadors serve in pulpits, but most are assigned to secular jobs. While still in his twenties, Beckett began wrestling with the implications of this reality in his own life. He recalls the struggle in his book, *Loving Monday*:

> I needed to know whether I should move into some form of direct ministry or stay in the workplace. After an extended time of searching, I sensed the Lord saying, "John, you are exactly where I want you." This settled the issue and I've had a great peace about what I'm doing ever since. We usually think of a calling in religious terms, such as a calling to the ministry. But a calling to a vocation goes beyond just the religious connotation. We can be called to the arts, to athletics, to government service or to business. If it is God's call, it is a legitimate and high calling. In other words, you can be an "ordained" plumber! People called to business have many opportunities for service unavailable to those who are specifically focused on ministry vocations.[4]

A necessary balance to obeying a call to business, Beckett says, is not moving forward independently from the One who issues the call. This is such a great tendency because entrepreneurs and senior executives come to their positions with all kinds of competencies. They have education, experience, and networks, but much of what they possess may not be aligned with spiritual truth. They need to think and act differently as believers. Rather than accept the prevailing wisdom, it is important to bring a spiritual perspective to day-to-day and long term issues such as relating to people, solving problems, and setting strategy.

Fortune magazine reporter Marc Gunther notes the difference between the spiritual and the secular approaches to business. "Marketplace pressures frequently bump up against spiritual values, as businesspeople tackle questions that reverberate beyond the bottom line: How to handle layoffs. How much to pay people. How to reach out to others in a loving way. How to react to unethical conduct. How to make money—of course—and make meaning, too."

Far from being marginalized, Gunther quotes Hamilton Beazley, a teacher at George Washington University, who says, "Spirituality is in convergence with all the cutting-edge thinking in management and organizational behavior. It creates a higher-performing organization."[5]

And the Beckett Corporation has been that, growing from a small business to the largest manufacturer of engineered components for heating systems in North America. Managing such growth has its challenges. Chief among them for John has been integrating his faith into every aspect of the business. "As part of our vision statement we say we are a biblically-based company. We communicate this to people as part of our new-hire orientation. During the process we share our corporate culture, our core values, and our desire to be guided by biblical concepts. We are up front about our desire to serve Christ.

"Some may question our forthright reference to biblical values," Beckett acknowledges. "For ourselves, we believe this emphasis helps set the boundaries within which we want to function. As we point out in explaining our corporate vision to employees, every enterprise is guided by some undergirding philosophy. Our management has elected to have biblical tenets and principles serve as that philosophy."

No place is this more evident than in John's dependence on prayer.

> Prayer is not often listed in books on how to run a business. But prayer has been a significant factor in our business, not only in the crisis, but as an ongoing process. For

over twenty five years I have met every Thursday morning with a small group of men. During these times we read Scripture, pray together and have breakfast. The prayer time often focuses on our work, including employee needs, wisdom in hiring decisions, insights into problems, and the need for clarity on important business issues.[6]

Beckett's sense of purpose remains strong as he nears forty years as CEO. "My job has given me opportunities to do much more than I could have in a traditional ministry setting for one main reason: I am where God wants me to be."

From cramped hospital rooms to cavernous government chambers, John Beckett exemplifies how believers should obey the call to be ambassadors of Christ. The appointment is a high honor. The assignment is to make a real difference wherever we are sent—including the workplace.

Other Voices

Through the years I have seen much fruit in the lives of business leaders as a result of meeting in small groups to talk and pray about life in general and their work in particular. These may or may not be church-sponsored groups. Sometimes it's just like-minded believers meeting regularly to discuss faith in the workplace, to give advice, to hold one another accountable, and to pray for each other. Such times can be very powerful.

John Bradley, founder of The IDAK Group

At a company I used to work for we did "Jesus Free Lunches" once a week for six weeks. We gave employees who came a free lunch— no strings attached. For the first week or two we did icebreakers and played games. We worked on building relationships and, in time, we earned the right to talk about the Lord with many who came. It's amazing what can be accomplished over a free meal.

Rob Strouse, former vice president of human resources,
United Support Systems

YOUR TURN

Create a library at your company stocked with books, tapes, and magazines that will enrich people vocationally, personally, and spiritually. Include a recommended reading list in your company newsletter. Write reviews on books that have impacted you and invite others to do so. Start a reading group at lunch and discuss books that address the larger issues of life, including a person's relationship with God.

Chapter Nine

Business As Stewardship

Commercial dealings are as old as civilization. Societies have always organized themselves into economic systems like capitalism or socialism or communism. ("The inherent vice of capitalism is the unequal sharing of blessings," said Winston Churchill; "the inherent virtue of socialism is the equal sharing of miseries.") Economists and philosophers argue about the best alignment of capital and labor and the means of production while wars are often fought to establish or preserve a particular set of market dynamics.

Much of the energy driving these global machinations comes from the desire to make money. "Ninety percent of the people in business believe their purpose is to make money for themselves and their shareholders," says Dennis Bakke, CEO of The AES Corporation. "I say no. Obviously you have to pay shareholders, you have to pay salaries, you have to pay taxes. But while this is part of doing business, it's not the main purpose. A corporation's goal should not be to make money, or create jobs, or be an instrument of the state. From my understanding, the purpose should be to use what it has been given to make the world a better place."

Bakke's philosophy doesn't come from his Harvard Business School education but from his commitment to Christ and his understanding of stewardship as taught in Scripture. Stewards today are associated with wine and horses. In biblical times, however, a steward was a "house manager," a chief servant put in charge of his master's property. When God created humans, He gave us dominion over the earth and charged us to care for His creation (see Genesis 1:26-30). That responsibility has never been revoked, and Bakke believes it applies to corporations as well as individuals.

Handle your corporate responsibilities as a sacred stewardship.

Bakke is a prime example of how a believer can shape a corporation to carry out a biblical mandate like stewardship. The start-up Dennis helped launch in 1981 is now a multibillion-dollar power company with fifty thousand employees serving a hundred and twenty million people worldwide. In 2000, they doubled their revenues to almost $7 billion while growing their asset base to $31 billion.

But money is not what turns the wheels at AES, as Bakke explains: "We don't use biblical words, yet our vision and values come from a biblical perspective, at least for me. Read Genesis and you'll find that our purpose in life should be to glorify God by stewarding the resources we've been given in order to meet the needs of others, and, along the way, to meet our own needs. To me, a corporation is just a group of people coming together to do the same thing. I believe the mandate to be good stewards is also a corporate responsibility, which may be the most unusual thing about AES."

Dennis is always up-front about his biblical worldview. He regularly lectures at such bastions of management education as Harvard Business School and Northwestern's Kellogg School of Business. Every new class starts the same way, with Bakke telling the students he is a follower of Jesus Christ and that what he does is motivated by his desire to live his faith with integrity. "I include the caveat that you can come at a life of integrity from different perspectives," he says. "My assumptions about people come from the Bible—every person is created with value; every person is unique; every person wants to make a difference—but these assumptions are consistent with what you find in most other faiths. Buddhists, Hindus, Muslims can buy into what we're doing at AES; everyone except a selfish humanist, that is. I also make it clear that the faith that motivates me is my own, not the company's. It is not a requirement that people share my Christianity in order to work at AES. However, they do have to adopt our way of doing business, and they should know that our corporate values are consistent with biblical faith."

His own journey of faith began with his conversion as a child, and has taken him in a different vocational direction from his evangelical family. There's no hint of rancor when he says, "I was sometimes called the black sheep because I went into the marketplace. My cousin was a missionary in Africa and both my brothers are ministers. In my background, if you couldn't be a missionary or a pastor you went into social work or teaching. If you had to go into business, you did so only to make money to support those in ministry."

This mindset is still prevalent in some evangelical churches, but Dennis doesn't buy it. He sees himself doing the same thing as his brothers, only in a secular setting. He points to Bible heroes like Joseph, Esther, Nehemiah, and Daniel—godly people who served in worldly places. "Most biblical heroes weren't priests or Levites," he points out. "Most weren't social workers or teachers; they labored in secular positions, and the same is true today. The marketplace isn't a bad place; it's the best place for most Christians to be."

To equip himself for his calling, Bakke earned an M.B.A. from Harvard Business School. After graduation he spent six years working for the government, then joined an energy think tank. In 1981 he hooked up with Roger Sant, a friend from government days, to start a business. "As I wrestled with what it would look like to live my faith with integrity in the workplace," Dennis recalls, "the questions came like a flood. How should faith affect company structure? How would it impact corporate governance? How could we create a fun place where people could use their gifts and skills to the maximum? I believed that work should be an expression of who people were and should give them the opportunity to do what God called them to do.

"This line of thinking led Roger and me to create an organizational structure that I believe is more biblically sound than any Christian organization I know of, not to mention secular corporations. We have no written policies to speak of, no handbooks, no human resources department, a microscopic legal office, and no finance department. And yet we've been very successful. When people see how well we've done and hear me talk about our purpose and principles, they say, 'Aahh, the new Harvard Business Technique!' Not at all. We've structured our company the way we have because we believe it better fits how people are supposed to live."

Organize your business to reflect your beliefs about God and people.

AES has such a high opinion of its rank-and-file employees that the company lets them make most of the important decisions. The board of directors primarily gives advice to others, including Bakke, who as CEO limits himself to making only a few organizational decisions a year. "Almost everyone is trying to become a businessperson instead of a worker," Bakke explains in the company's Annual Report for 2000. "At the core of making our employees independent businesspeople is our fun value and our goal to create the most fun workplace ever. We have become convinced that the central condition required to create a fun working environment is allowing the maximum number of individuals to make important decisions regarding any and all aspects of the company's business. We are trying to change the Industrial Revolution mindset typified by this quote ascribed to Henry Ford: 'Why is it that I always get a whole person when what I really want is a pair of hands?'"[1]

This handing over of power to subordinates is difficult for many executives, Christian or not. Its prototype can be found in the Bible, which instructs leaders to serve others rather than to be served. Perhaps that's why the management symbols Dennis has chosen for his office are a sculpture of Jesus washing Peter's feet and a picture of Mother Teresa.

Because of what he believes about God and people, Bakke has helped create an organizational structure like no other in the secular or nonprofit world. Its value-driven, decentralized approach has been tested in the crucible of crisis. When AES had major problems over falsified plant reports in 1992, Bakke almost lost his job. "I was the number two man at the time, but I was the one most identified with the values we were trying to live by. The board felt there was something wrong, and everyone on Wall Street blamed our crazy management system. Some people said we were too 'faith-based.' They wanted to change the values and return to a more conventional organizational structure. It was a scary time. A lot of people rallied around me and we hung onto our original vision and values. We made it through and a couple years later I became CEO."

The struggle over how core values shape corporate structure can be a recurring battle. It has resurfaced at AES in the wake of the terrorist attacks of 9/11. Dennis once more faces the same pressures he did a decade ago, and this probably won't be the last time his vision will come under fire.

High-profile faith has some unique challenges. Christians are held to a different standard, no matter what their titles. That's why a lot of Christians are afraid of putting their faith out there. They don't want the added accountability. Bakke's own style has been to be both visible and vulnerable. "Christians need to acknowledge that we make mistakes. We're just as fallible as anybody else. Even though we aspire to higher principles, we are going to fail at times. We may be redeemed, but we're still sinners, just like everybody else. It's humbling yet true.

"At AES, we want our people to bring their faith—whatever it is—to work with them. Instead of saying, 'this is business and it has its own set of rules,' we want them to be the same people here they are in their homes and in their places of worship. Everybody likes that part; but when we turn it around, they're not as excited. We also want them to live by these principles the rest of the time. We care if someone cheats on his spouse, or on her income taxes. It's just as bad as cheating in the workplace. There shouldn't be two sets of rules for life. This is what we mean by integrity."

Model integrity in your personal and public life.

As time-consuming as running a multinational corporation can be, Bakke tries to model what this kind of integrity looks like. He serves as director of Young Life of Washington, D.C. and is a board member of the Council for Excellence in Government. He and his wife, the former Eileen Harvey, started the Mustard Seed Foundation in 1983 to better steward the resources of the Bakke and Harvey families. Inspired by the parable of the mustard seed in Mark 4, the foundation provides grants to churches and Christian organizations worldwide. In 2000 alone, they awarded over $7 million in grants, with two-thirds of the funds going outside the United States.

From the beginning of AES, Dennis has tried to stimulate others to invest in worthy causes. As part of its social responsibility, the company matches employee giving to nonprofit organizations, including churches and religious organizations. The goal is to give 5 percent of after-tax profits. AES contributed over $20 million through this program in 2000, just over 4 percent of after-tax profits. This money isn't given to salve a guilty social conscience or to buy good press. Rather, it's a way to recognize and encourage personal social responsibility. Dennis stresses that charitable acts like the matching gifts program "play only a small role in fulfilling our total responsibility to society. Our mission to serve the world with safe, clean, reliable, and reasonably priced electricity is a more important focus than the wonderful charitable acts we undertake. Serving the world with electricity and other services is our ultimate responsibility. It's the stewardship we have been given."

"Now it is required that those who have been given a trust must prove faithful" (1 Corinthians 4:2). According to *The Expository Dictionary of Bible Words*, the Greek word for faithful means "an unshakable loyalty, which is displayed in a number of ways. We see it in the faithful servants of Matthew 24:45 and 25:21-23, who prove trustworthy in carrying out their assignments. 'Faithful' is also a word used to commend believers for their quality of steadfast endurance" (1 Corinthians 4:17).[2]

For more than twenty years, Dennis Bakke has "carried out his assignment" through the company he helped create. His words and work are Christ-honoring, yet have been discussed in many secular venues from *The Washington Post* to *The Harvard Business Review*. While most believers won't have this kind of global impact, we all have this kind of personal obligation to be good stewards.

What a solemn responsibility.

What a great privilege.

Other Voices

I had lunch one day with a colleague who showed no interest in spiritual matters. Since it was near Easter I used this as a starting point to learn of his religious background. I asked if the Resurrection had any significance for him. He said it didn't, so I took a "what-if-Christ-really-rose-from-the-dead" approach that got him thinking. I've found that by making "what if" statements and asking others to, "just imagine if it were true," I can speak good news to people without offense.

Scott White, former financial planner,

Penn Mutual Life Insurance

One day during a presentation in my store, a jewelry salesman used "Jesus Christ" as swear words. I responded, "Oh! You're talking about my friend." Immediately he apologized. Later, over lunch, I was able to share what it meant to have a personal relationship with Jesus. He told me it was the first time in his sixty-plus years anyone had ever talked to him about trusting Christ, and he thanked me.

Bob McNicol, president of Timmreck & McNicol Jewelers

Your Turn

When employees retire or leave the company, take the opportunity to thank them for their services—either in person or in a letter—and wish them well. As they look ahead, ask them also to consider what comes after death. They have probably spent years preparing for the time between now and the grave; invite them to spend a few hours thinking about eternity. As a going-away present, give them a book or booklet that clearly explains how they can find eternal life.

Chapter Ten

High (Tech) Calling

High-tech companies are a recent phenomenon in the long history of commerce. Much about them, from the incredible pace at which they operate to the high profits they can generate—and lose—is different from other businesses. Managing the accelerated rate of change has become the key to survival according to Andrew Grove, former head of Intel:

> Businesses are about creating change for other businesses. Competition is about creating change. Technology is about creating change. The appearance and disappearance of regulations cause further changes. Sometimes these changes effect only a company; other times they effect an entire industry. So the ability to recognize that the winds have shifted and to take appropriate action before you wreck your boat is crucial to the future of an enterprise.[1]

The lightning speed and sudden shifts on this roller coaster create high G-forces and vertigo. Those who sit in the front cars are most susceptible to losing it. Christian executives in the computer, dot-com, and techno-entertainment industries are as much at risk as their peers. However, they have access to the antidote for anxiety disorders as prescribed in Philippians 4:6-7: "Do not be anxious about anything, but in everything, by prayer and petition, with thanksgiving, present your requests to God. And the peace of God, which transcends all understanding, will guard your hearts and your minds in Christ Jesus."

Set your heart on serving Christ; let Him pick the location.

Christians in high stress environments can do more than survive; they can help others find calmness in the chaos and meaning that goes deeper than money. As marketplace Christians, they are called to work among people who have dismissed the church and clergy as out of touch with the real world. For many years, Greg Newman has served Christ in Silicon Valley, the epicenter of the computer culture. In addition to starting some very successful companies, he has held senior positions at Apple and Oracle. A believer in Jesus from childhood, Greg got serious about his faith in high school and decided to become a missionary. He went to Moody Bible Institute in Chicago to prepare for overseas service. He never finished his degree in theology but left after a year and a half. "I moved back to California in 1984 to marry my best friend," he recalls. "I planned to return to school, but we began having kids and I decided to start a business instead."

Newman opened the first desktop publishing company in Silicon Valley in 1984 at age twenty-two. Through the business he met some influential people from Apple Computer. He wound up going to work for them two and a half years later. After a few exciting years he moved on to do marketing and sales for a start-up called Macromedia.

Macromedia took off and quickly grew to six hundred employees. It helped define multimedia for the computer industry and achieved dominant market share in multimedia authoring. After Macromedia went public, Newman began casting around for a new challenge. He found it in a start-up called New Video. The company had backing from Apple and Intel, but hardware problems and a shortage of capital torpedoed the venture. "This was my first real failure in the computer industry," says Greg. "I thought it might be time to sell everything and go to the mission field. I still had a heart for missions and couldn't quite understand how I wound up in Silicon Valley. I felt very torn and prayed about it constantly. I told God I would leave everything if He wanted me to. But every time I looked overseas, the doors slammed in my face. So I stayed in business and tried to do the best job I could."

After the failure of New Video, Greg was out of a job for several months. He still remembers it as a very painful time. "I kept thinking, I don't know if I want to do this again, but God led me back into computers. Apple asked me to be the senior product manager of the QuickTime team. We worked very hard and established QuickTime as the standard in cross-platform system-level multimedia software. Then Apple had a downturn and I moved over to Oracle as the senior director of product management for their New Media Division. Later, I helped start the Internet group there and experienced a lot of success."

As a senior exec at a high profile company, Greg was at the top of his game. Yet all was not well in the land of Oracle. The company is known for its cutthroat corporate culture. The reputation is accurate, according to Newman. "I found myself in an environment where my honesty and integrity were constantly challenged. Everywhere I went in business, I made it known that I was a Christian. This served two purposes: it told people what my life was all about, and it held me accountable to live up to my faith. My testimony was always on the line. But this was the first place people took advantage of my being a Christian. Time and again I got stabbed in the back. People stole my ideas and represented them as their own. Being a believer made it difficult to advance, yet God faithfully protected me. Where somebody meant something to harm me, it often wound up being for my good. This only reaffirms how important it is to walk with integrity, no matter what the setting."

Not that Greg has been perfect. "I've certainly had times of compromise in my career," he admits. "I wasn't always consistent. I screwed up and I made mistakes. I've had tests of my integrity that I failed. But through it all I've matured as a person and as a businessman. The trials I experienced at Oracle were just a part of the process."

Establish a vibrant counterculture if your environment is hostile to Christianity.

Greg eventually left Oracle to start C2B Technologies with Scott Walchek, a friend from the Macromedia days. "There were no other Christians at Macromedia," says Newman, "and I felt like a lone light until Scott came on board to head up marketing. I knew the moment I met him there was something different about this guy. Over dinner at a trade show several weeks later I asked him about his life. He looked at me and said, 'My life is based on the Word of God. I'm a Christian and I love Jesus Christ with all my heart.' For the first time I felt like I had a brother in the company. We became good friends and Scott became my mentor. He's an excellent example of a man of God who is also a well-respected and influential executive."

C2B Technologies became their attempt to create a company based on Christian principles and characterized by integrity. Greg and Scott made a commitment to found the company on prayer. They met every morning with a few other Christians who came to work for them.

While prayer was a key commitment, they didn't write it into their corporate mission statement. "We didn't think this was appropriate because we were raising public monies," says Newman. "We also didn't want employees to feel like they had to pray or be Christians to work for us. Still, everyone knew we were believers and we didn't hesitate to talk in company meetings about how God was answering prayer. We gave honor to Him in everything we did."

The culture at C2B differed from its techno-neighbors in ways other than a dependence on prayer. The founders did not want people to sacrifice their families on the altar of Mammon, the reigning deity in Silicon Valley. Investment consultant Michael Stolper once described the perfect fund manager as "a guy who can't pick his kids out in a police lineup." The saying also applies to software developers and systems engineers, but Newman didn't want it to apply at C2B. "We expected people to work hard, but we also realized there was more to life than work. If someone needed to be at his son's Little League game, he could go. We encouraged our folks to take vacations. We did not push for eighty-hour weeks, although there were times when we needed to put in some long hours and everybody was willing to do that. However, we tried to make this the exception and not the rule. It was amazing the number of family people we attracted because of this practical aspect of our Christian worldview."

This kind of concern ran counter to Valley culture, described by author and social critic Paulina Borsook as including beliefs such as: "Technology is the solution to all human problems. The market is the true test of everything. Money is the highest good, and, all government and regulation is bad. There is an overbalance on the spreadsheet way of knowledge, which says that if it can't be quantified, then it has no value." She goes on to show how these beliefs produce a stockholder theory of value wherein a company's highest priority is now perceived to be to its stockholders, not to its customers, and certainly not to its employees or community.[2]

As company founders, Newman and Walchek set a different tone at C2B by their example. To their times of prayer and their practical concern for families, they added an insistence on integrity in all business dealings, especially with financial backers and strategic partners. "It's not the norm to be completely aboveboard in this very competitive market," Greg admits, "but we believed we could compete fairly and vigorously from a position of consistent honesty and integrity. There were times that severely tested our resolve, but we stayed true to our original vision."

Whether for an entire company, or a small department, executives have to model the values they want to see in their people. Robert Haas, CEO of Levi Strauss, once told the *Harvard Business Review*:

> The first responsibility for me and my team is to examine critically our own behaviors and management styles in relation to the behaviors and values that we profess and to work to become more consistent with the values that we are articulating. It's tough work. We all fall off the wagon. But you can't be one thing and say another. People have unerring detection systems for fakes, and they won't put up with them. They won't put values into practice if you're not.[3]

Be accessible and open with people; don't become isolated by your position.

One of the most important truths Greg has learned from Scott through their close working relationship has been not to set himself up as untouchable. The tendency of some CEOs is to separate themselves from everyone in the company, which Greg says is unwise. Being one of the guys, however, can sometimes put Christians in difficult situations, as Greg knows all too well. "There are times when you're at lunch or out with people and they're drinking and partying; that's not the image Christians want to present. There's a real art to knowing when to make a strong statement about your faith and when to put people at ease and not make them feel like you're coming across as holier than thou.

"We didn't preach at C2B," he continues. "We just lived our lives in front of our employees. I know they respected us because we still get calls from people saying, 'I just want you to know that my time at C2B was the best work experience I ever had. I want to work for you if you ever start another company.' What impressed them was Christ in us. It was His character shining through and certainly not our charming personalities."

God blessed this desire to honor Him, and C2B expanded rapidly. In 1998 the company was sold for $132 million shortly before the steep rise in Internet stocks, which took the value of that acquisition to over $2 billion at its height. Since the sale, Greg has divided his time between his duties as a general partner of Integrity Partners, a venture capital firm investing in high-tech start-ups, and his work with EquipNet. EquipNet is a nonprofit organization Newman started to provide Internet-based technology solutions and training to Christian leaders around the world. "As the western mission movement passes the baton, a new generation of missionaries is emerging," Greg explains. "Indigenous leaders know how to reach their own people and present Jesus in the most relevant ways. And they can do so for a fraction of the cost of the traditional missionary. Through EquipNet we want to be a catalyst to bring resources to this very strategic group."

Newman's involvement goes far beyond funding. He has traveled to several countries and is actively engaged in developing the software and technology needed to make EquipNet work. This hands-on participation puts Greg among the investors that Scott Kirsner, editor for *Wired*, calls:

> [T]he new breed of high tech philanthropists [who] want to reinvent the art of generosity. They share [the] sense that simply giving money away is too passive and uninvolved. They want to lend business expertise, identify and support social entrepreneurs hungry to shake up the non-profit world, and quantify their results. In short, they want to create a new kind of charity. But they don't call it that. They call it venture philanthropy.[4]

Greg's two loves—ministry and technology—have been joined in a fruitful marriage. "EquipNet is an absolute thrill," he says, "because I can take the assets and experiences I've gained through my business career and apply them to expanding God's work around the world. I realize now that God did give me a call to missions as a young man; He just wanted me to take the high-tech road to get there."

The "missionary" calling is not to a location but to a lifestyle. The first missionary Jesus sent to the Gentiles was told, "'Go home to your family and tell them how much the Lord has done for you, and how he has had mercy on you.' So the man went away and began to tell in the Decapolis [his home area] how much Jesus had done for him. And all the people were amazed" (Mark 5:19-20).

Like this nameless disciple, our most effective ministry will probably be among our families and work associates. And if we serve faithfully close to home, who knows where we might end up.

Other Voices

I have had the opportunity to head up a number of nationally prominent organizations with large numbers of employees. Upon taking these positions, one of the first things I do is have an all-employee meeting, teleconferencing in all the branch offices. The first statement I make is, "I want you to know that I am a Christian. I will always try to function as a Christian in my decision-making and in my relationships with you." This forthrightness has always opened doors for me and I have never had one complaint.

Dick Schultz,
former executive director of the U.S. Olympic Committee

Good Friday is not observed by any of our customers or suppliers in the telecommunications industry. Our usual policy is to be open when our customers are open, but I decided long ago to honor this sacred day by being closed. Each year I send out an e-mail explaining from the Bible what happened on that first Good Friday and what it means to me.

Paula Mann, CEO of Sunbelt Telecommunications

YOUR TURN

Stressful circumstances create openings to display God's love in practical ways. According to the Holmes-Rae Stress Scale, the most stressful life events are: physical suffering, grief caused by the death of a loved one, marital difficulties, financial pressures, and problems with children. If you know people who are undergoing any of these, tell them you are praying and are available to help them find the resources they need. Be prepared to follow through if they take you up on your offer.

Chapter Eleven

Family Litehouse

Many businesses start out as family affairs. They range in size from small farms to the biggest corporation in the world, Wal-Mart, but still share certain characteristics. At the outset they are based on relationships, not bureaucracies. Their value systems are understood and don't have to be spelled out in mission statements. Authority and responsibility reside with the founding father (or mother), and are usually conferred on a chosen heir at the time of succession.

When the family is overtly Christian, this unity of structure and purpose gives weight to their testimony. The business is seen as an expression of their faith in God and their desire to do good to others. However, if the relatives are selfish or hypocritical, this alienates nonChristian employees and customers, and also embarrasses other believers who work there.

Founding family members don't have to be perfect, but they have to relate to one another with the sharing, bearing, forgiving, kind of love outlined in 1 Corinthians 13. If their prayers and practices are in alignment, and their words and works in sync, they can build a successful business with a God-honoring reputation. Doug and Edward Hawkins

Jr. have done just that with Litehouse Foods. Their flagship salad dressings are the second most popular retail refrigerated dressings in the country, and the main reason why company sales reached $70 million in 2001. These brothers took the answer to their father's prayer and turned it into an international brand. In doing so, they have become one of the largest employers in Bonner County, Idaho—a family responsibility they take very seriously.

Acknowledge answers to prayer as a means of drawing attention to God.

The roots of the Hawkins' family business go back to 1949 when Edward Sr. worked at a restaurant in Spokane, Washington. The owner was unhappy with the salad dressing, and one night Edward came up with a unique bleu cheese dressing as an answer to prayer. He took the recipe with him to Hope, Idaho when he bought the Litehouse restaurant in 1958 and featured it alongside other homemade specialties. Word spread and customers began bringing jars to take home the dressing.

In 1963, Hawkins began selling product to local grocers, and soon the whole family was "in business." Sons Doug and Edward Jr. were in charge of packaging and distribution. "We were making the dressing in the restaurant kitchen," Edward Jr. remembers. "Whenever a waitress or busboy had a free moment they would come in and help. Our delivery truck was a Datsun pickup with a camper shell. During the winter we had to wrap the boxes of dressing in sleeping bags to keep them from freezing."

"The restaurant was really struggling in the early '70s," says older brother, Doug. "We used the dressing to supplement the business. My parents and I were praying about what we should be doing, and the answer we received from God was that it should be something beyond just meeting our own needs. It should also involve providing jobs in our community in an environment that expressed and supported our faith. We didn't know it then, but the salad dressing, and not the restaurant, would be the fulfillment of our prayers."

When the Hawkins family decided to make salad dressing their primary focus, business improved. By 1974, annual sales approached $100,000. They jumped to $250,000 by the end of the next year and to $1.5 million by 1977 when Edward Jr. came on full-time. Litehouse Foods moved into their own building and kept expanding. Today, they're the second largest employer in Sandpoint, Idaho, just down the lake from Hope. Doug heads sales and marketing, while Edward Jr. directs operations and finance. Their payroll of four hundred people—working in two facilities and outside sales—is the fruition of their family prayers. They have a corporate mission statement now, which includes being a good employer and contributing to the economic base of the community.

Being able to provide neighbors with a livelihood is a wonderful privilege and many business owners testify to the joy it brings. Robert Stover, founder of Westaff, Inc., among the largest temporary staffing companies in the world, says, "One of the great feelings of accomplishment I have is knowing thousands of people in America and hundreds overseas are making a decent living because of us. They are able to raise their families and live their lives in a quality way. Creating jobs is one of the great gifts an entrepreneur can give to the world." Jackie Baca, CEO of family-owned Bueno Foods, seconds the notion. "When you create jobs, you give people an opportunity to better themselves. Work gives people dignity and the means to improve their lot in life. What a noble calling!"[1]

"We are responsible for our people," says Edward Jr. "We want them to know we take this responsibility seriously because of our Christian faith. During the daylong orientation we conduct for new hires each month, Doug and I take time to share the Litehouse story. We explain that we are Christians and that this is a Christian-based company. We emphasize that they don't have to be Christians to work here, but they need to know who we are and where we're coming from. Then we share a little about our history, including that the recipe for our original bleu cheese dressing came to our father as an answer to prayer."

As a leader, exemplify a high-profile, low-pressure approach to faith.

While Christianity is front and center at Litehouse, it isn't forced on anyone. "Edward and I have not pushed Bible studies or prayer meetings at work, although we have participated in both ourselves. But neither have we discouraged any group that wants to have studies. We open our sales meetings with prayer and make Christian literature available throughout the organization."

"At times we might invite an employee to attend an outside event like Promise Keepers," Edward Jr. says, "but it's always their choice. There's no pressure. Our temperaments are such that we don't pressure people. We both have fairly quiet personalities."

This high-profile, low-pressure approach has borne fruit through the years. Doug tells the story of one man who came to Litehouse in 1975. "He knew we were Christians and he wasn't interested, until about a year and a half ago when he finally became a believer. He's on fire for the Lord now. Obviously, this is not how it always turns out. Through the years we've hired people who didn't live up to our expectations. We are both ex-coaches and educators, and when we made mistakes it's usually that we coached too long when we should have cut people. At the same time, we don't know how we touched their lives while they were here."

"Had we been at the level of management experience we are now," Edward says, "we probably could have made many of those folks successful. Who knows?"

Christianity at Litehouse is also expressed outwardly in the emphasis Doug and Edward Jr. put on community involvement and customer service. Their philosophy on the latter is simple; the customer is always right. "We want to provide the best service we can because our faith calls us to be servants," Edward explains. "If a customer calls in a late order, for instance, we will make sure that it gets out overnight at no extra charge."

Through the years, grocers and produce managers have rewarded this commitment to service with increased business. In the late 1980s Litehouse expanded their product line and added a food service division. Consequently their brand is in stores from east to west and on tables from north to south.

More important to the Hawkins brothers than their growing national reputation is the respect of their neighbors. "What strikes me most about Doug and Edward Jr. is their humility," says local business owner Don Otis. "They support the community in ways that even local people don't know about. Litehouse also employs hundreds of residents and treats them very well. I've never heard anyone complain about how they were treated at Litehouse. People around here respect the company for its success, and those who know the Hawkins family understand it has a lot to do with their faith."

Show a steady dependence on God in good times and bad.

The clear sense of direction at Litehouse stems from the Hawkins' commitment to Christ. The business began with an answer to prayer and continues in that same spirit of dependence. That's why it has been able to survive some heavy blows. "The restaurant was in bad financial shape early on," Doug remembers. "We had a person go south with a bunch of our money, yet we didn't believe in quitting or filing for bankruptcy, so we just struggled through. In 1974, Dad got sick and had to spend the summer in the Veterans hospital. Edward came back from a summer job to help me and that's when we decided to make Litehouse our careers. We had the debt to deal with and had to buy jars and ingredients on a weekly cash basis for the next week's production."

"Any entrepreneur is going to face struggles," Edward warns. "The critical thing is to keep your faith through the tough times. It's what will get you through the good times as well. The basis of our faith is the conviction that we are doing God's will. Because of this confidence we can take every aspect of our business to Him in prayer. We pray at sales meetings and at company picnics and dinners because this makes a statement about our trust in God."

Doug adds, "Our faith also gives us a basis upon which to make business decisions. We try to lead by example and to teach our employees to do the right thing because it's the right thing. You can make a bunch of rules, but every rule has an exception. However, if you do what's right because of your beliefs and your integrity, that's honoring to God."

It also happens to be good for business in most instances. However, that's not why people of faith do what they do. In the book *Built to Last*, which the Hawkins brothers cite as being instrumental in their thinking the last few years, former Stanford Business School professor, James Collins, and the school's associate dean for academic affairs, Jerry Porras, show the significance of identifying and remaining consistent with core values. These they define as "the organization's essential and enduring tenets—a small set of timeless guiding principles that require no external justification; they have intrinsic value and importance to those inside the organization." They cite the following as examples of value-driven companies:

> Subservience to the customer as a way of life at Nordstrom traces its roots back to 1901 — eight decades before customer service programs became stylish in business. Bill Hewlett and David Packard held respect for the individual first and foremost as a deep personal belief; they didn't read it in a book somewhere or hear it from a management guru. Ralph Larson, CEO of Johnson & Johnson, put it this way: "The core values embodied in our Credo might be a competitive advantage, but that is not why we have them. We have them because they define for us what we stand for, and we would hold them even if they became a competitive disadvantage in certain situations."

"The key point," Collins and Porras conclude, "is that an enduring great company decides for itself what values it holds to be core, largely independent of the current environment, competitive requirements, or management fads."[2]

For Doug and Edward Hawkins Jr., the core is Christ, or, as Jesus Himself put it: "I am the vine; you are the branches. If a man remains in me and I in him, he will bear much fruit; apart from me you can do nothing. . . . If you remain in me and my words remain in you, ask whatever you wish, and it will be given you. This is to my Father's glory, that you bear much fruit, showing yourselves to be my disciples" (John 15:5, 7-8).

Doug and Edward Jr. have tried to glorify the Lord in their life's work, which puts them in a long line of brother-disciples that began with the apostles. (The Twelve included two sets of brothers — Peter and Andrew, and James and John — who worked together in a family fishing business.) Looking ahead, Edward says, "We know we won't be around forever. Most of our management group has been with us for quite a while. They know how we think, they know what we believe, and they have been trained to make decisions the same way we do. We feel good about the company's future being in their hands."

"We have been so blessed in blessing others," says Doug. "We want the blessing to continue long after we're gone. We want the stewardship of this company to outlive us."

So do their hundreds of employees and millions of customers.

Other Voices

Christian executives should know how to use prayer to change things — and people. Once a coworker got very upset about the work habits of another employee. He had shared his concerns many times with the troublesome person, who promised to change but never did. I startled my coworker by asking, "Have you been praying for this man?" Together we agreed to pray daily for him. Within a few weeks, the employee's behavior improved so dramatically that it was blatantly obvious to the whole work group, prompting many to ask me what management technique I had applied. This gave me an opening to share my faith.

Eddie Filho, manager of IT services, FedEx

On a recent plane trip I struck up a conversation with my seatmate. I asked what he did for a living and we discussed the latest news. Soon I used my favorite transition question to see if he was open to spiritual things: "Do you have any kind of spiritual belief?" This is the first of five questions I learned from Bill Fay's *Share Jesus Without Fear*. I was able to get through the questions with this man and share from my pocket

New Testament. Fay's simple approach has helped me to discern when the Lord is opening someone's heart.

David Simonds, branch manager, Flair DataSystems

YOUR TURN

Put items in your workspace that will make others curious about your faith: a Bible on your desk, awards and letters of appreciation on your walls. If you have a life verse, put it on a plaque. If you have bookshelves, display the works that have helped you grow personally and spiritually. Have books or booklets available to give to those who want to know more about what makes you tick.

Chapter Twelve

Living On-Target

The first law in Bill Bright's classic booklet, *The Four Spiritual Laws*, says: "God loves you and offers a wonderful plan for your life." Through His prophets, Jehovah often told His chosen people that He had marvelous plans for them. "'For I know the plans I have for you,' declares the Lord, 'plans to prosper you and not to harm you, plans to give you hope and a future'" (Jeremiah 29:11). The New Testament apostles also confirmed that God has a plan for each believer (see Ephesians 2:10; Titus 2:14).

This isn't some sort of hard-wired determinism. People can exercise their option as creatures to disobey; consider Jonah. But God can exercise His right as Creator to intervene in their affairs; consider Jonah. Finding and fulfilling our God-ordained purpose is like bringing a character to life on the stage. The Divine Playwright has scheduled our entrance and exit and given us a role to play (see Psalm 139:13-18). How we develop our characters is largely up to us. We can try to discern what the Director wants and let that influence our performance, or we can ignore Him and ad lib.

Choosing to follow the script isn't restrictive or robotic. Rather, it's tremendously encouraging to know we have a part to play in a larger story. We are important to God; what we do in our daily lives matters to Him. It also impacts those around us.

No one believes this more ardently than Albert Black Jr. Whether it's running his business, On-Target Supplies & Logistics, serving as chairman of the Greater Dallas Chamber of Commerce, or loving his wife and three kids, Albert knows what he's doing—and why. He was born the youngest of seven children, and raised in the tough Frazier Courts housing projects in South Dallas. What he lacked growing up was minor compared to what he had—a praying grandmother and a persistent faith in God.

Leverage your successes into greater opportunities to share Christ.

"I've always known who I am and whose I am," says Albert. "I was raised in a Christian home and have never not known Jesus. My grandmother was a great influence on me. I can still remember waking up as a child and seeing her reading the Bible in that beautiful rocking chair of hers."

Growing up in the projects, Black believes, gives one a certain perspective, a paradigm with a very low baseline. But he refused to accept the limitations of his environment and chose instead to conquer them. The civil rights movement was beginning to have an impact during his childhood and he witnessed an unprecedented exodus from the ghettos by black people. It left him with an extraordinary appreciation for the American free enterprise system. "The idea that a young person, no matter their starting point, could put their hopes and dreams to work and make something of themselves was exciting to me as a little boy," he recalls. "Sure, I was born in the projects, but I was never allowed to think like I was poor. God blessed me with the ability to see challenges in ways that caused inspiration rather than resentment. By the time I was ten, my friends and I had started Best Friends Lawn Services. We borrowed the old rotary mower from the Frazier Courts' office and went door to door to find customers. That's how I got started in business and I've never looked back."

Albert attended Eastern New Mexico University on a football scholarship and later was graduated from the University of Texas at Dallas in 1982. That same year he and his wife, Gwyneith Navon Black, started On-Target Industrial Maintenance. The two-person, part-time, custodial company has grown from annual revenues of $10,000 to $40 million today. In 1992, On-Target quadrupled its warehousing capacity by moving to an inner-city business district in South Dallas, from which it now serves clients throughout five states.

Their success has given the Blacks the chance to share their faith with a growing circle of people that includes employees, clients, and neighbors. "Show me your faith without deeds," challenges James, "and I will show you my faith by what I do" (James 2:18). What Albert, as CEO, and Gwyneith, as vice president of business relationships, are doing is helping a whole lot of folks lead more productive lives. "On-Target's mission," say the founders, "is to develop a company of well-trained, highly-motivated, customer-service-oriented professionals. In addition, we want to improve the tax base and infrastructure of the inner city by hiring tax-users and turning them into tax-producers. We are making a difference in our neighbors' lives and building better communities in the process. Our employees, as a group, contribute almost one hundred hours a month to community activities, which includes serving on more than twenty boards and commissions."

As a CEO, Albert knows he has a responsibility to run a profitable company. "But you also have to do what's best for people," he adds.

"You can't just say, 'Well, it's business and I don't have any responsibility for what happens outside of work.'" Leading by example, Albert has served as chairman of the Greater Dallas Chamber of Commerce's board of directors. He was also the first African-American to be president of that body. His community contributions earned him the Ernst and Young Entrepreneur of the Year, Community Service Initiative for a Competitive Inner City Award, in 2000.

Choose the platform for service from which you can be the most effective.

The Blacks have great respect for the local church and are active members of New Hope Baptist Church. But you won't find Albert in the pulpit. "I'm not a theologian, so you're not going to see me preaching," he says. "I'm a businessman, so I choose those platforms from which businessmen can be effective. I don't waste my time trying to do what others are better trained to do. Instead, I focus on being the best at what I'm trained at. My job is to create enterprises that can employ people, improve infrastructure, generate taxes, and provide leadership in the community. That's my ministry.

"One of the most rewarding things about what I do is having people look me in the eye and say, 'If it weren't for this company, I wouldn't have the life I have.' Creating opportunities for people who otherwise would have none, that's doing God's work."

The fingerprints of faith are all over On-Target. Take the Friday morning staff meeting for instance, which begins with a prayer session. "We have Muslims and Buddhists and Jews who work here," explains the CEO. "We love the diversity of our company. Ethnically we are 60 percent African-American, 30 percent Anglo, and 10 percent Hispanic. Anyway, during this prayer time most of us pray silently, but I know that we are all praying for the same things all good people pray for. We pray for peace. We pray for guidance. We pray for dependence on God and independence from evil. We pray for help in reaching the goals we have as individuals and as a business."

This prayer time illustrates the balance Albert strives to maintain between his overt Christianity and the value he places on diversity in the workplace. He knows what racism and bigotry look like, and that neither has anything to do with the gospel. Shaking his head, he says, "Discriminating against people because I am a believer in Jesus Christ and they are not seems to me like blowing up bridges versus building them. How could I say I encourage diversity at work while being a religious bigot at the same time? I have to embrace my Jewish friends and employees, and my Islamic friends and employees.

"Christian CEOs have to use their position and authority to resist bigotry," Black continues. "I've seen the type of isolationist thinking Christians sometimes bring to work, which is nothing more than religious prejudice. Faith becomes another reason to discriminate against people, another reason for not liking someone. Believing executives can help prevent this by creating environments where tolerance is valued and modeled."

But this doesn't mean watering down personal faith. Albert says, "People don't want you to water down your faith. When you do that to accommodate others in the name of getting along, what you end up with is not much of anything. Christians need to be bold about what we believe, but we also have to be careful not to come across like John the Baptist. We need a different brand of ministry in the workplace, a ministry of performance. We have to earn people's respect by our actions before they will listen to our words. If we want to really help others, we have to take a personal interest in their lives much like Jesus did. So often, executives hide behind their positions and remain impersonal. But if we're going to help others become better businesspeople, better family people, and ultimately, because of these things, to become Christians, we have to encourage them to change. And people change when someone cares about them personally."

Exceed people's expectations, and give the credit to God.

"There is no question that race remains one of the biggest barriers to communication and trust in the workplace," says Black. Yet he freely admits that one of the reasons for On-Target's early success was because they were being used to demonstrate that racism wasn't a problem in Dallas. "Companies hired us, then turned around and boasted, 'See, we don't have a race problem.' But on our side of the equation, we've had to overprove, overprove, overprove. We've had to dispel the myth that minorities can't do the job with an exhibition of excellence and the consistent delivery of value—not only for our customers, but for our employees, our partners, and our financial backers."

Unfairness is part of life on planet Earth, as Albert understands better than most. "In any economy, there's going to be discrimination, and race is one of the easiest ways to do so. Until we get to heaven we have to accept the fact that there will always be limited resources and unlimited demand for them. Some form of discrimination usually determines who gets what. The issue for me is: What am I going to do about it? Like my father used to say, 'Okay, so the coach doesn't like you. Okay, so the teacher is giving you a hard time.' He would never argue with me on that. Instead he would say, 'Now that you know this, what are you going to do about it?' That same question applies to me as a businessman. Now that I know that minorities in business are discriminated against today, and will be tomorrow, what am I going to do about it?"

His strategy has been to exceed expectations at every level, starting with the basics. Black's creed, influenced by fellow entrepreneur Bob

Buford, is simple. "When you say you're going to do something, do it. When you have an appointment, show up on time. When anybody does anything for you, say 'thank you.' And when somebody helps you, always ask, 'What can I do for you?'"

"The color of my skin has never been a barrier to performance or success inside of me," says Herman Cain, chairman of Godfather's Pizza and the first African-American president of the board of the National Restaurant Association, "but it's sometimes been a barrier to others around me. Performance that exceeds expectations is the best response to ill-informed attitudes."[1]

Racial myths exist on both sides of the color line. Albert mentions one he knows quite well. "There is a myth that African-Americans can't own businesses or lead effectively. If you've never seen something before, you may not believe it's possible. Many of our employees have never seen a successful African-American business owner. They've never seen African-Americans who are competent and comfortable with leadership responsibilities. That makes me feel inspired, challenged, and blessed to have the type of job I do."

Black's business and community successes have resulted in his being selected by the mayor of Dallas as a "Top Talent" professional. He's won the 30th Congressional District Award for outstanding achievement in business and received the Quest for Success Award from the Dallas Black Chamber of Commerce. When asked how a kid from the projects could accomplish so much, he replies, "How could I have not done it? I've got an extraordinary faith in an awesome God. I believe His promise that everything will be all right if I trust Him. That makes life easy for me."

"The first principle of ethical power is Purpose," write Ken Blanchard and Norman Vincent Peale. "By purpose, I mean your objective or intention—something toward which you are always striving. Purpose is something bigger. It is the picture you have of yourself—the kind of person you want to be or the kind of life you want to lead."[2]

Albert Black has always known the kind of person he wants to be. At forty-three—the midway point of an average life—he's living out his dream every day. "I've been blessed with a clarity of faith that has never wavered," he says with deep gratitude. "God has called me to be an entrepreneurial leader in the communities of which I'm a part, and I know that what I'm doing is making a difference. Not just for today but for eternity."

"Not that I have already obtained all this, or have already been made perfect," Albert would agree with the apostle Paul, "but I press on to take hold of that for which Christ Jesus took hold of me. Brothers, I do not consider myself yet to have taken hold of it. But one thing I do: Forgetting what is behind and straining toward what is ahead, I press on toward the goal to win the prize for which God has called me heavenward in Christ Jesus" (Philippians 3:12-14).

That's what it means to be living On-Target.

Other Voices

After I became a Christian, I shared the gospel with my sister. She believed in God, but didn't want to commit her life to Him yet; she was still young and having too much fun. I bought some roses and let them sit until they were good and wilted. Then I gave them to her and said, "I've had these for a few weeks and they're ready for the trash, so I decided to give them to you." She was offended, until I explained, "Now you know how God feels about you wanting to keep the best years for yourself and offering Him what's left. Besides, you never know how long you will live. Why take the risk?" Shortly after that she accepted Christ.

Mike Hamel, coauthor of *Executive Influence*

When I worked as an administrator for the University of Massachusetts, I was surrounded by faculty, staff, and students from around the world. I often asked people why they dressed or acted or expressed their faith certain ways. My genuine interest was often reciprocated. I was frequently asked about my actions and personal faith. This exchange of experiences and ideas proved a great benefit to me and allowed me to talk about God with people who might never visit a church. I'm convinced that more people would listen to what Christians have to say if we listened before we spoke.

Paul Regan, former administrator, University of Massachusetts

YOUR TURN

Encourage a faith-friendly environment at work by having written guidelines for religious activities. A simple list of do's and don'ts can free people to be more open about such things. Having your board, legal department, and HR people scrutinize the guidelines should stimulate good discussion and allow you to articulate your own understanding of the role of spirituality in the workplace.

Chapter Thirteen

Doctor's Advice

Some professionals wield great authority even though they don't preside over large bureaucracies or multimillion-dollar budgets. These include doctors, lawyers, pilots, and other highly skilled people who routinely assume the responsibility for the well being of others. While some are drawn to these occupations by the money or the prestige, others go through the rigorous training and take on the enormous stress that comes with life-and-death decisions because they want their lives to make a difference.

Christians in these vocations have a unique opportunity—and a solemn responsibility—to share the good news when appropriate. So says Dr. David Parsons, a world-renowned pediatric otolaryngology surgeon. "I believe Christians who are executives, entrepreneurs, or professionals like myself have been extraordinarily blessed. Scripture teaches that those to whom much is given, much will be expected."

Parsons has never been one to shrink from responsibility. After being drafted in 1966 he joined the Air Force and became a fighter pilot, winning the Top Gun award in three different fighter aircraft, including the F-105 Thunderchief, at that time the fastest low-altitude fighter in the world. He went on to fly more than 450 combat sorties during the Vietnam War. "Tom Wolfe wrote a book about fighter pilots called *The Right Stuff*," Parsons recalls with a smile. "He talks about the enormous egos of fighter pilots and says that no other professionals have egos to rival them except surgeons. The same week I won the Top Gun award in the Thunderchief, I was accepted into medical school. I went on to graduate from the University of Texas, and completed both a pediatric residency in San Antonio and an Otolaryngology/Head and Neck Surgery residency at the University of Colorado."

After twenty-six years of military service, Colonel Parsons retired in 1993. He is in private practice in Greenville, South Carolina, where he's also a clinical professor at the University of South Carolina. He has earned the respect of his peers and his patients, and has been named among the top one thousand doctors in America. What excites David now is the ministry he has with those who come to see him every day.

Don't hesitate to share the spiritual solution to life's problems with those who ask.

"I am blessed by having people with needs sit in my office and wait for me to say something important," Dr. Parsons muses. "It's the perfect context to explore not only the physical, but the spiritual dimension of life. I don't try this with every person, but there are those who clearly have a need that transcends the physical. If I ignore the spiritual, I cannot cure that patient. For them, I take the time to ask, 'Are you in a stressful situation right now? If so, what are you leaning on to help you through this period?' After they answer, I say, 'Can I tell you how I would deal with something similar?' Then I might share a one-minute version of my testimony, emphasizing that when I was in a stressful situation I learned to lean on God through faith."

Is it proper for physicians, or other professionals, to take advantage of someone's pain as an opening to share the gospel? Certainly it would be unethical to exploit a patient, or a client, for personal gain. But it would also be unloving to leave out what could be part of the solution to their difficulties. Parsons insists that doctors should not ignore the spiritual side of life. "Say you have bad sinuses and come to me with a physical complaint. How could there be a spiritual part to your sinuses? Well, I know that one of the major causes of sinusitis is the reflux of stomach acid. And the reflux of stomach acid is caused by emotional stress. If I ignore the emotional stress causing you to reflux, and I only treat the physical, then the reflux is not going to be well managed. This means I can't make you well. So I have to transcend the physical and get into the spiritual if I'm going to be an effective doctor."

Parsons is not alone in this conviction. Researchers Richard Cimino and Don Lattin comment:

> Doctors are sold on the physical benefits of faith. A 1996 survey of members of the American Academy of Family Physicians reports that a remarkable 99 percent think religious faith helps patients respond to treatment. The study, conducted by Yankelovich Partners, found that most of these doctors thought spiritual techniques should be part of formal medical training, and 55 percent report they use these techniques as part of their current practice. In fact, the spirituality-health connection is finding a place in medical education. The National Institute for HealthCare Research reports in 1997 that nearly one-third of American medical schools offered courses on spirituality and healing.[1]

What about the people who are not interested in spiritual advice but just want the healing or legal counsel they came for? These services should be rendered as effectively as possible, and without reference to religious sentiments. Christian professionals need to do what they are being paid for, "as unto the Lord." But even when a No Trespassing sign is posted, the sensitive believer can still plant seeds. Dr. Parsons does this by talking about how he has learned to handle his own stress through dependence on God.

Use your own story to "gossip" the gospel.

People who have been Christians for a long time often forget the life-changing impact of their own conversions and so lose the passion to introduce others to Christ. But Dr. Parsons can still remember what it felt like to be on top of the world outwardly—and desperately lost. His longsuffering family put up with his drive, which kept David going non-stop. David's wife was a Christian, but when she shared her faith with her husband, he showed no interest. "In my situation," he recalls, "everything looked good on the surface. But inside, things were in shambles. My wife, Begee, kept praying for me, and a friend talked me into joining a small fellowship of men. Through their kind words and patient friendship, I opened my heart to Jesus Christ. Slowly, peace, contentment, and joy began to fill me. Since then, my story only gets better. My life now centers on a daily walk with Christ that affects every decision I make. And one of the most important decisions is to share my faith whenever I have the chance.

"From the beginning of my conversation with someone," Parsons continues, "I want to know about the five 'Ws', who, what, where, why, and when. 'What is your family like? Where are you from? Tell me about your home, your parents.' When it's appropriate, I ask about spiritual things in a nonthreatening manner: 'Did you go to church as a child? Did you grow up in a Christian home? Do you pray?' As I get to know them, I begin to sense where they are spiritually and what their needs are. I look for a point of contact with my own experience as an open door to share the Lord. It takes a conscious obedience to the Holy Spirit to direct the conversation to spiritual issues. If you just wait for it to flow freely on its own, it may never happen."

David encourages Christians to have several versions of their personal testimonies ready to share at a moment's notice. He himself has a thirty-five-minute talk, a five-minute version, and a one-minute summary. Each explains how everything seemed perfect for him, how it crashed, what led to the crash, what kind of lessons he's learned, and continues to learn, through it all. At the urging of a mentor, David prepared a tape of his conversion story and has been able to distribute almost a thousand copies through the years. He carries tapes with him and regularly finds occasions to give them to those he meets.

David finds opportune moments to share his faith and love on the way to the operating room. "I try to have physical contact with the patient, whether that's holding their hand or even their foot, being especially careful if the patient is a woman. I say, 'Can I tell you what I did this morning? I prayed for you.' I don't say, 'I am going to pray for you.' I make it past tense. I say, 'I have prayed for you.' I also tell them I will be praying while I'm operating. Then, one of three things happens. They either give me positive feedback, which leads me to say, 'Would you like to pray together before we go into the operating room?' Or, I get a cold, flat response, to which I make no further comment. The third option is somewhere in between, and I ask the Lord for wisdom as to what to do. I have never received a negative response to my approach. Rather, I get a tremendous number of letters from patients, even from those who gave no favorable response, saying they really appreciated the prayer." He adds,

"I did have a Jehovah's Witness tell my nurse that she knew I prayed for my patients, and she didn't want me to pray for her. That is the most negativity I've ever received. On the other hand, I have learned from the questionnaire patients fill out when they come to my office that a reasonable number of them are here because they heard I pray with my patients."

Even when people are open, Christians should still be careful about how they proceed. In their book, *Show and Then Tell*, Kent and Davidene Humphreys pass along some fatherly advice from a man whose son took a job on a church staff as director of evangelism. The father was a nonChristian, who nonetheless wanted his boy to be a success in his new job. So he called and gave three suggestions on how to relate to people:

1. Treat us like people, not projects.
2. Take time to teach us clearly. We don't understand your big religious words like sin, grace, and repentance. We can't put our faith in Christ without the facts.
3. Do not be rude. Talk lovingly. Let us control the conversation. You can control the context.[2]

Learn from your mistakes, and expect God to use you in spite of them.

Amidst the positive spiritual experiences he's enjoyed, Dr. Parsons has had his share of failures. At one time he thought it would be a good idea to do a Bible study in his office. When he announced to the staff that every Monday morning they would start the day with a Bible study for anyone who was interested, the decision produced anger and resentment. Some couldn't come because of children; others felt left out. "In retrospect," he admits, "I should have asked the staff individually if they were interested instead of just making a pronouncement."

Dr. Parsons has also been frustrated when talking with his peers. "I don't know why this is. I am very effective with patients, nurses, and technicians. But doctors are so busy; they have very little nonmedical time to go beyond surface conversation. However, there are exceptions. I once had a competing surgeon ask for help with his terrible sinus problems. What a humbling thing for this doctor to come to me. And as he sat pinned to my examining chair with a telescope up his nose, I began asking him questions and getting to know him as a person instead of a competitor. 'Isn't it amazing,' I said, 'that we men can talk about business and sports, but we never get to the harder things. Women can sit down and share everything with each other, including what's deep in their hearts. Men never do that. I'll tell you why. It's because we're afraid we will say something that will cause the other person not to respect us.'

"I went on about how men never get together to discuss the important issues of life. Then I told him about the men I met with on Thursday mornings. I invited him to join us. Not only did he come, he became a Christian as a result. He still meets with the group. He is grow-ing by leaps and bounds, and we have gone on five missions trips together."

These missions trips take Dr. Parsons all over the globe, includ-ing back to Vietnam and Cambodia where he now helps the people he once tried to destroy. Personally and professionally, David is a new man with a new mission. He is following the practice of the Great Physician who cared for both body and soul. Jesus never imposed on those who came to Him for help, yet He never hesitated to address the spiritual issues behind surface problems.

Physicians are an extreme example, but most professionals have a certain amount of credibility by virtue of their expertise. Most want to provide quality service to those who seek them out. And what better service could be given than to point the way to eternal life?

(If you would like a copy of Dr. Parson's story on tape or CD, write to him at parsonsdav@aol.com.)

Other Voices

For years my wife and I wanted to share Christ with our neighbors but never did, until we attended a conference where the concept of evangelistic parties was presented. As a result, we hosted our first neighborhood Christmas party. After singing and games, we asked our guests to share their thoughts and memories of Christmas. I then shared our experience of knowing Christ as Savior. They responded with delight. After the holidays we began a home Bible study, and three neighbors trusted Christ. When we were transferred to Dallas, we continued having parties and hosting Bible studies. In three years, over sixty neighbors became believers, and from that beginning has grown a church of over twelve hundred "neighbors."

Norm Wretlind, former regional sales manager, Grolier, Inc.

When I become aware of needs in people's lives, I ask if I can pray for them. If they say yes, I invite them to the table in my office. I don't pray over my desk at them, but side by side with them. I pray because I believe God is present and interested in their lives. The prayer is always simple and conversational. While I ask people if I can pray for them, I wait to be asked to share the gospel. When people express an interest, I'll talk to them freely about Jesus Christ.

Mike Haddorff, president, Collins Control & Electric

Your Turn

Look for occasions to give away copies of the New Testament or the whole Bible. Possibilities include: new-hire orientation; exit interview; retirement; as a reward for exceptional service; during times of bereavement; or as gifts for birthdays, weddings, or anniversaries. If this would violate company policy, give them as personal gifts. Write something on the flyleaf—a favorite verse, a prayer—to make the gift more personal.

Chapter Fourteen

Little Rewards, Big Rewards

B ack in A.D. 610, an Italian monk decided to reward his students by baking scraps of leftover bread for them. He twisted the dough to resemble his students, who folded their arms across their chests when praying. He dubbed the snack pretiolas, meaning "little rewards" in Latin.[1]

The most famous *pretiolas*, or pretzels, in America today are the creations of Anne and Jonas Beiler of Auntie Anne's. From a stall at the farmers' market in Downingtown, Pennsylvania, their business has grown to more than seven hundred stores employing more than ten thousand people worldwide. The Beilers never set out to build an international company; they just wanted to provide free counseling to hurting families in their community. This desire grew out of having their own marriage restored through the loving intervention of a Christian counselor. God has rewarded their passion with a ministry exceeding their wildest dreams.

The most effective witnesses are those who share from personal experience. The people Jesus healed were among His most ardent evangelists (see Luke 8:1-3; John 9:25-33; 1 John 1:1-4), and it remains so to this day.

Be a conduit of the grace of God you have received in your own life.

Anne Beiler was born and raised in the Amish culture of Lancaster, Pennsylvania. While still a child, her family changed to the Amish-Mennonite church. This meant they had electricity on their farm and a car—it had to be black. "Mom and Dad loved us eight kids and taught us about God," Anne says. "At the age of twelve I accepted Jesus Christ as my savior when an evangelist came to our church."

Anne met and married Jonas Beiler when she was nineteen. Life was good until their middle child, Angela, was killed in a tragic accident shortly before her second birthday. Anne was devastated. "For the first time I questioned everything I had been taught about God. I went down a very dark and troubling path for the next ten years. My despair almost ruined our marriage. We were on the verge of divorce."

When the Beilers moved to Austin, Texas, they met a Christian counselor who helped them save their marriage. "Jonas and I became excited about helping other couples make it through tough times," Anne says. "We started to do some marriage counseling in our home and it became a real passion for Jonas. In 1987 we returned to Pennsylvania because we felt we needed to minister to the Amish and Mennonite people. Jonas began dreaming of building a huge counseling center in Lancaster County. 'How do you think you're going to do this,' I asked him, 'especially without charging people?' He said, 'I don't know, but God will provide for us.'"

Once they got settled, Jonas started counseling three days a week, studying two days, and working one day. After about six weeks, Anne decided to go to work to help support their vision. "From day one, the purpose of Auntie Anne's has been to support our passion to help families," she says. "Jonas is a very quiet man, but he loves deeply and has great compassion for people. Doing whatever I can to help him is a big part of my mission in life."

Anne took a job as a store manager at a farmer's market in Maryland. Seven months later, in February of 1988, she got a chance to buy her own store in a Downingtown, Pennsylvania market. Sensing God's direction, she borrowed $6,000 and bought the business, sight unseen. "This is not how you should do things," she says wryly, "but I really felt the Lord wanted me to buy the store. My motto has always been Psalm 32:8, 'I will instruct you and teach you in the way you should go; I will counsel you and watch over you.' He has truly instructed and led us. Our business grew from that one store to where Jonas and I were managing eight stores by ourselves. In 1990 we started to franchise, and today we have over seven hundred stores.

"I have always known what our purpose is," Anne continues. "It is to give. I understand giving in terms of giving our lives to God first. If this commitment is real, it will involve our business and our money. We give more than twenty percent of net income. This hasn't changed as our revenues have increased. In 1992, we were able to open the Family Resource and Counseling Center. Plans are in the works for developing a center for every fifty to one hundred stores as we continue to expand. We also give substantially to The Children's Miracle Network and other ministries."

God smiles on such principled generosity, but banks don't. When Auntie Anne's tried to borrow money in 1993, the banks said no. The problem wasn't with company net income, but with charitable outflow. The ratios were upside down, but the Beilers weren't about to change. Soon the Lord led them to a local chicken farmer who liked their pretzels and their principles. Over coffee and a handshake they struck up a financial partnership that lasts to this day.

This scenario has been repeated a few times since with bankers and venture capitalists. The Beilers have turned down large infusions of money whenever compromises were attached to the cash. And God continues to bless the business and the ministries it supports.

Refuse to let the fear of man silence you.

For the Beilers, business and ministry aren't separate activities. "Many people don't go to church, but they do go to work," Anne observes. "And this is the perfect place to minister to them. In the beginning I wanted to hire only Christians so I could say we were a Christian company. Now I say we are Christian-owned company based on Judeo-Christian values. Today we ask prospective employees how they feel about working for such a company. We explain our values and code of ethics, and let them know what we expect as far as behavior. We've never had any problems with this openness; it's always been a plus. Even our vendors and suppliers tell us how refreshing it is to work with people doing business in this manner.

"We have prayer at many of our meetings. When I'm present, I share something that God has done for me lately. I've never had anyone express unhappiness about this. At our annual conventions I always share with our franchisees the ways God has been faithful to us as a company. I give Him all the glory. I don't use my platform to directly evangelize people, but I do speak openly about God's goodness and love. I'm a firm believer in walking before talking. As Christians, if we live our lives as unto the Lord, this will create opportunities to share. To be salt, you have to be tasty. To be light, you have to shine. I've always said, 'Light shines, it doesn't speak.' Our statement of purpose is summed up in the acrostic LIGHT:

Lead by example,
Invest in employees,
Give freely,

Honor God,

Treat all business contacts with integrity.

In talking with her peers, Anne has learned that some executives don't talk about God in the workplace because they're afraid of being sued for religious discrimination. Others are frustrated at being warned not to antagonize anyone. "When we started Auntie Anne's, people told me not to put my Bible on my table because it might offend people. They said someone could actually take me to court for it. At first I was paralyzed. 'God created this company,' I told myself, 'yet I can't even put His Word on my desk!'

"It took me a while to thaw out and realize that I certainly have the right to talk about my God in the workplace. I came to the point that if it meant that Jonas and I would have to defend ourselves in court for talking about the Lord or praying at work, we would gladly do so. Christians should not be afraid. God works in the presence of faith, not fear. Fear is the realm of Satan. To live in the realm of faith and to walk the talk is our Christian responsibility."

Beiler's voice goes up a notch when she says, "I don't understand how a Christian can be in business and not have God at the core. I know some people try to separate their business and personal lives, but I think they're one and the same. If you are a Christian, God is with you. How can you not take Him to work?"

Anne feels as deeply about being called to business as a missionary feels about being called to another country. "This is where God wants me to influence others for Him. Running a company is just as important as pastoring a church. I can't see any difference. One time I was with a missionary who said to me, 'I get embarrassed at church when they parade the missionaries up front and tell everyone how much good we are doing. I look back at the congregation and think, look at all these business-people. They are the ones who should be up here.' He has a good point."

Anne's sense of calling was sorely tested in the early years of business. "When we came back from Texas, we weren't thinking 'business'; we were thinking 'ministry.' We started Auntie Anne's to support our counseling work. As the company grew, I got busier and busier. I told the Lord how frustrating this was to me. We had been called home to minister, and now I was so busy that Jonas and I could no longer co-counsel with couples. Then one Sunday at church I was crying during the worship service. 'I came home to do ministry,' I told the Lord. 'Have I gotten off track somewhere?' Then in my mind I saw myself standing in front of Jesus rolling pretzels. And it was the most amazing revelation! I felt Him telling me He wanted to use Auntie Anne's as a vehicle for His work. Wow! And from that moment on, I've set my heart on ministry in the workplace. That was over twelve years ago, and I'm still inspired by what I get to do. Every step of the journey has been so exciting and we've only just begun!"

Keep an eye on the rewards Jesus promises for faithful service.

Jesus once told His disciples, "No one can serve two masters. Either he will hate the one and love the other, or he will be devoted to the one and despise the other. You cannot serve both God and Money" (Matthew 6:24). However, it is possible to use money to serve God, which is what the Beilers are doing. The reward for doing well in business is profit, which in turn can be invested for even greater rewards.

C.S. Lewis astutely pointed out that there are different kinds of rewards:

> There is the reward which has no natural connection
> with the things you do to earn it, and is quite foreign

to the desires that ought to accompany those things. Money is not the natural reward of love; that is why we call a man mercenary if he marries a woman for the sake of her money. But marriage is the proper reward for a real lover, and he is not mercenary for desiring it. . . . The proper rewards are not simply tacked on to the activity for which they are given, but are the activity itself in consummation.[2]

The reward Jonas and Anne get for their labor is the ability to touch people through Auntie Anne's, through the Family Resource and Counseling Center, through the Angela Foundation, through their sponsorship of the Children's Miracle Network, and through the personal impact they are having on those around them. As Anne likes to say, "We give, to get, to give again."

"Whatever you do, work at it with all your heart," Paul commands in Colossians 3:23-24, "as working for the Lord, not for men, since you know that you will receive an inheritance from the Lord as a *reward*" (emphasis added). Thinking about rewards isn't selfish; it's spiritual. The Beilers are turning the "little rewards" of business into "big rewards" for the future, which is exactly what Jesus said to do:

> "Do not store up for yourselves treasures on earth, where moth and rust destroy, and where thieves break in and steal. But store up for yourselves treasures in heaven, where moth and rust do not destroy, and where thieves do not break in and steal. For where your treasure is, there your heart will be also." (Matthew 6:19-21)

Other Voices

Each month for ten years I wrote a letter to our employees. I wrote of everyday subjects from a biblical perspective but without using religious language. For twenty-five years I also sent a Christmas letter to our suppliers and customers relating a real-life experience to God's gift of His son. One July I was visiting a buyer's office and he pointed to last year's letter pinned to his wall. "I reread it often," he said. "It helps me get through the day." By writing about life in a candid way, I've been able to share with all sorts of people, many of whom have trusted Christ after years of patient interaction.

Kent Humphreys, former CEO,
Jacks Merchandising and Distribution

Our customers are made aware of our faith through our mission statement, which is printed in our catalogs and posted on our website. We also sponsor a prayer gathering at our biggest industry trade show to which we invite customers, associates, and competitors. Every year we organize and underwrite a Community Leaders' Breakfast. We bring in a high-profile speaker who happens to be a Christian, asking the person to challenge the audience regarding leadership, and then share his or her testimony.

Darrell Schoenig, founder, Ultimate Support Systems

YOUR TURN

Plan time in your schedule each month to take a colleague to lunch or dinner. Go as couples if this is more appropriate. Extend the invitations to those who show an interest in spiritual matters. Keep the setting relaxed and try not to discuss work. Show an interest in their personal lives. If the subject comes up, be ready to talk about the Lord, but don't push.

Chapter Fifteen

Crisis Management

The prolific philosopher, Anonymous, once wrote that "adversity introduces a man to himself." It also introduces a company to its CEO and other executives. Corporate calamities test the mettle of mission statements and take the moral measure of those who occupy the head office. Sometimes the crisis is internal, as in the case of the Enron and WorldCom meltdowns. Other catastrophes come from outside and strike with the impact of a plane crashing into a building.

No incident in recent memory has been as unexpected or disastrous as the September 11, 2001 terrorist attacks on the World Trade Center and the Pentagon. Individuals, families, companies, cities, the whole world, have been forced to stare into the unblinking eyes of evil. Our hearts have been broken along with our sense of security.

While the scope of human wickedness can be overwhelming, Christians are not to be overcome. "Because the days are evil," Paul warns believers to "be very careful, then, how you live—not as unwise but as wise, making the most of every opportunity" (Ephesians 5:15-16). No sane person looks forward to crises. However, when the inevitable does come, Christians are to respond differently than those who have no hope, since "we know that in all things God works for the good of those who love him" (Romans 8:28).

Believers have a sacred duty to share this hope with the hurting. Thousands did so in the wake of September 11, including executives like Merrill Oster, whose New York offices are a few blocks from Ground Zero.

Merrill is the founder and CEO of Oster Communications, a group of companies that currently includes Oster Dow Jones Commodity News and FutureSource. The former provides commodity news to traders and risk managers, while the latter provides online futures prices and analysis to a wide range of clients. More than two hundred and fifty thousand brokers, money managers, and traders rely on Merrill's companies for real-time information. More than two hundred and fifty employees have come to rely on Merrill personally for inspiration and assistance, especially during tough times.

Be God's hands and feet during times of crisis.

Merrill was in London when terrorists attacked the United States and took almost three thousand innocent lives. He returned home and gathered his family for a tearful time of hugs and prayers. The following Monday he was in New York to do the same with his business family. Going from office to office, he tried to reassure his traumatized staff. He brought in grief counselors to help them cope with the aftermath of the disaster.

In a letter sent company-wide, he shared the perspective that buoyed him through his own loss of friends and associates.

> As I sort things out, I take comfort in this nation's spiri-
> tual heritage for strength and direction. This event is a
> fresh reminder that this world is only a temporary resi-

dence for me and you. Every nation and people has some concept of God. The one I have chosen to follow is the God of all creation, and His Son, Jesus, whom He sent to pardon my and your sins and make it possible for those who accept His free gift of salvation, to have a peace that exceeds all understanding in this tumultuous life, and eternal life when we leave this world. . . . It appears that our nation, and many throughout the world, may be turning back to God as the ultimate source of good. Light extinguishes darkness. Good will ultimately win over evil.

This wasn't "God language" rolled out when nothing else seemed appropriate; it was the expression of a lifelong faith. Employees, clients, and friends know of Merrill's faith and his spiritual approach to life's ups and downs. "I believe God speaks through crises and that we should see such times as opportunities to get serious with Him," Oster says. "It's His way of telling individuals or companies, or even countries, 'Let me have your attention; it's time for a course correction.'"

Merrill had other opportunities to share his faith while in New York. One evening he took some employees to dinner, and as they were talking about what had happened, a man walked up and said, "I'm sorry for eavesdropping, but when you're done, would you mind coming over and talking to us?"

"The same thing had happened to me the night before," Merrill says. "I was with a consultant friend and he was telling me his story, where he was when the planes struck, how he escaped. He said he planned to move his family out of New York. 'That's an interesting response,' I said. 'As a Christian, I believe my times are in God's hands.' That opened up a conversation and I gave him a Bible. And while I was taking him through *The Four Spiritual Laws* booklet, a couple at the next table said, 'We'd be happy to buy you a drink if you'll let us talk about these things with you.' It was absolutely spine tingling!"

"Be wise in the way you act toward outsiders," counsels the apostle Paul, "make the most of every opportunity. Let your conversation be always full of grace, seasoned with salt, so that you may know how to answer everyone" (Colossians 4:5-6).

The "answer" carries more credibility when the one giving it speaks from personal experience. Christians who have seen God deliver them through their own trials know the reality of the hope they are sharing, as Merrill can testify. His company went through its biggest crisis during the agricultural depression of the middle 1980s. When the bank called his loan, precipitating a cash emergency, he called his executives to his home for a time of prayer and planning—a practice that continued for several months. Then he went to his department heads and confessed, "I've put this company in jeopardy because I've been too aggressive financially. We're up on the high side; we could crash if we don't take some immediate action."

This candor helped build a closeness that is still part of the culture at Oster Communications. It also extended to those outside the company. "I went to our major suppliers and told them we couldn't pay our bills as timely as we had in the past," Merrill continues. "I asked for their patience and help. Out of a dozen suppliers only one said no. With their understanding, and a bridge loan, we were able to pull through."

Trials come our way to test and season our faith (see Romans 5:3-5). Philip Yancey suggests that mature faith doesn't look around and ask, "Why me?" Rather it looks ahead and asks, "To what end?" This positive approach to negative situations is possible because of the hope of the gospel. "When those who work for me ask how I can be so optimistic," says Merrill, "my answer is, 'I've read the end of the book. I know how it all turns out.'"

Live with the confidence of one who has a divine calling and destiny.

Oster's unshakable optimism grows from a personal faith reaching back to childhood. "I heard the claims of Jesus Christ from my parents and grandparents, and at the age of thirteen, I received Him as my Savior. My family never segregated their Sunday activity from their Monday activity, so I grew up thinking it was normal to serve God in every situation."

That's why as an adult, Merrill never thought to exclude God from the dozen or so businesses he has started since graduating from college. His life-mission is reflected in the mission statement of Oster Communications: "We exist to serve God by nurturing our people, to help our customers manage financial risk, to build a solid global information services company, and to pursue excellence in everything we do."

Given this devotion, one might think this Iowa farm boy would have grown up to be a preacher. However, Merrill had a different calling. While attending the graduate school of journalism at the University of Wisconsin, he discovered the financial and influential power of timely information. Learning everything he could about subscription-based publishing he launched Professional Farmers of America in 1973 and went on to start several other successful companies under the Oster umbrella.

Merrill went into business because he felt it was where he could do the most good with his life. "Near the start of my career, I was selected by members of the Iowa Republican Party to be groomed as a possible future governor. I felt honored by their interest, but told them that while there were a few hundred people who could walk that path, I had a higher calling: business ownership. This is where God wants me to be. As an owner-executive, I can honor my Lord by promoting godly vision and values through my companies."

This prerogative of ownership has been challenged on occasion. Oster has had employees express concern over the influence of his Christianity on company operations. "When someone questions the propriety of how I apply my faith, I take it as a teachable moment and say, 'I welcome you here and I appreciate your concern. But when you came on board, you could tell our vision and values were biblically based. You knew you would be working for a Christian CEO. I'm not trying to force my faith on you, but I'm so excited about what I have that I want others to know about it."

Merrill believes that executives create natural opportunities to share the gospel by being up front about their faith. He illustrates with the following story. "I remember a guy who had been with us for about six months. He was close to my financial dealings and knew I drove a hard bargain, but he also knew I gave away a lot of money. He expected a hard-bargainer to be a greedy son of a gun. One day he walked into my office, sat down, put his feet up on my desk and said, 'Oster, there's something different about you. Do you mind telling me what it is?' This gave me the chance to tell him about Jesus Christ. After we talked awhile I asked him if he wanted to receive Christ—and he did, right there in my office!"

When executives establish an open environment by the values they profess and by personal example, it encourages others to talk about philosophical and religious issues. That's very rewarding to Merrill, who says, "If I can create a culture where people feel comfortable talking about the real issues of life and how faith applies to them, that's powerful. I'm not responsible to talk to everyone. I just need to speak when the Lord gives an opportunity and to encourage others to do the same."

Do something to improve the world your grandkids will inherit.

"As CEOs and entrepreneurs, we have spent a lot of time in our companies and communities," Merrill says of himself and his peers. "We have built up a reservoir of influence. As we reach our fifties and sixties, we come to the equivalent of harvest time on the farm. We should ask ourselves how we can best use this stockpile of influence to help others. That's what I'm trying to do through Pinnacle Forum."

Pinnacle Forum has grown out of Merrill's interaction with other concerned believers. The nonprofit organization based in Phoenix encourages highly influential Christians to reach their peers with the gospel. They also equip these "cultural gatekeepers" to work toward rebuilding America's moral foundation. "Forty years ago there was a 'common sense' about right and wrong," says Merrill. "Today no such understanding exists. As a result, standards are disappearing and moral decay is eroding our society. There is a direct connection between America's abandonment of Judeo-Christian morality and her cultural decline."

Robert Bork came to the same conclusion regarding this country's problem and its solution. In *Slouching Toward Gomorrah*, a scathing critique of modern liberalism, he wrote:

> Whether the link between religion and morality can be demonstrated conclusively, as I have come to believe it can, it is true that the coming of trouble in our culture coincided with a decline in the influence of religion. . . . Only religion can accomplish for a modern society what tradition, reason and empirical observation cannot. Christianity and Judaism provide the major premises of moral reasoning by revelation and by the stories in the Bible.[1]

Bork, former Solicitor General and U.S. Court of Appeals judge, has seen firsthand a myriad of social ills multiplying like weeds in American soil that has been spiritually sterilized. Looking to the future he says, "Perhaps the most promising development in our time is the rise of an energetic, optimistic, and politically sophisticated religious conservatism. It may prove more powerful than merely political or economic conservatism because religious conservatism's objectives are cultural and moral as well."[2]

Pinnacle Forum is an active expression of that religious conservatism. It is an attempt by Oster and others to reverse a decline that he admits, "happened on our watch. While we were busy growing our businesses and raising our families, the values of our country went down the tubes. Now that we're at the peak of our influence, we need to use that influence to make a difference for the sake of our grandchildren. We need to improve the world they will inherit."

"With God's blessing and strength," Merrill wrote in his post-9/11 letter, "we can build a better, more thoughtful, more spiritual America out of the ashes of the World Trade Center, the Pentagon, and the field in Pennsylvania. It was over that field that a few Americans, led by Wheaton College graduate Todd Beamer, overwhelmed the terrorists and prevented a plane from hitting yet another target, and perhaps saving even more innocent people. One person, doing what he or she can do, can make a difference."

Thousands of people risked their lives on September 11 to save others. Hundreds paid the ultimate price for their heroism. In a broken world where evil abounds, Christians have a similar opportunity—and responsibility—to show the Way to the lost, the Truth to the seeker, and the Life to the dying. The greatest service we can do for people in crises is to introduce them to the One who said, "I am the resurrection and the life. He who believes in me will live, even though he dies; and whoever lives and believes in me will never die" (John 11:25-26).

Other Voices

We sometimes sit around the table at the firehouse reading the morning paper. Recently a crewmember remarked about the dismal state of the world. We spent forty minutes discussing the Middle East and other trouble spots and I was able to bring up Christianity's message of hope in this natural setting. As a supervisor, I have to be careful about initiating spiritual conversations, but talking about the news is something everybody does.

Dean Folkerts, lieutenant, Colorado Springs Fire Department

After selling my company in 2000, I called about forty former employees and invited them individually for coffee or lunch. All accepted. At the meetings I asked permission to share my spiritual values. Billy Graham's tract, *Steps to Peace with God*, was my guide. I invited each one to receive Jesus Christ as Lord and Savior. About 25 percent did so and another 25 percent who didn't pray expressed interest in learning more. I gave them each *The Daily Walk Bible*, plus the Jesus video and encouraged them to call me with any questions. Once I was no longer "the boss," I found I could freely share without my former position getting in the way.

Chris Crane, coauthor of *Executive Influence*

YOUR TURN

If you're not already part of a peer group where you can pray and talk about what's going on in your life, why not join one? Check with your pastor or Christian colleagues to see if they know of a group that would fit you. Or, contact Fellowship of Companies for Christ International at 800-664-3224 and ask if they have a group meeting near you.

Appendix

Christian Rights in the Workplace

(This material was excerpted with permission from the booklet, *Christian Rights in the Workplace: What the Law Says about Religion at Work*, published by The American Center for Law and Justice. The ACLJ is an international public interest law firm specializing in constitutional law.)

Introduction by Jay Alan Sekulow, chief counsel, The American Center for Law and Justice

There will always be opposition to the spreading of the gospel. Some in our society want religious people to keep their convictions to themselves and leave their religion at home. The law, however, does not require that religious employees and employers check their religion at the office door or the factory gate when they come to work.

Federal and state laws protect the religious freedoms of employees and employers. Employers can run their business in conformance with godly principles and employees cannot be forced to act in a manner that conflicts with their religious beliefs. For instance, Christian employers may hold and participate in voluntary chapel services and prayer meetings for employees, and employees can share their faith with coworkers during breaks or free time as long as it is not disruptive.

For the business world to act ethically and responsibly, it must have access to sound religious morality through its people in ownership as well as on the work floor. More people are being made aware of this truth and have decided that, despite pressure from society, they can no longer keep their faith a secret while at work. After all, if we have sincerely committed our lives to God, how can we leave Him out of the place where we earn our living and spend the better part of each day?

Employer Religious Beliefs

Many employers have sincerely held religious beliefs which they want their businesses to reflect. But federal and state laws prohibiting religious discrimination in employment have discouraged many business owners from communicating their religious convictions at work. The good news is that, just like employees, business owners do not have to check their religion at the door when they come to work. The following information provides some guidance for religious employers who want their business to reflect their faith.

Q.   Do employers unlawfully discriminate if they base business objectives and goals upon biblical principles?

A.   No. An employer does not discriminate on the basis of religion by affirming the faith of its owners in business objectives.[1] "Title VII does not, and could not, require individual employers to abandon their religion."[2] Employers must be careful, however, not to give prospective or current employees the perception that employment or advancement with the company depends on acquiescence in the religious beliefs of the employer. This can be accomplished in a number of ways. For instance, applications for employment should state that applicants are considered for all positions without regard to religion. This statement should also be included in any orientation materials, employee handbooks, and employee evaluation forms. Of course, employers must also be sure that this statement is accurate by not discriminating on the basis of religion.

Q.   As the owner of the business, can I witness to my employees?

A.   An employer can talk about his religious beliefs with employees as long as employees know that continued employment or advancement within the company is not conditioned upon acquiescence in the employer's religious beliefs. For instance, one court has held that an employer did not discriminate against an employee by sharing the gospel with him and inviting him to church.[3] Employers must be careful, however, not to persist in witnessing if the employee objects. Such unwanted proselytizing could be deemed religious harassment. Employers cannot impose their religious beliefs on their employees.[4]

Q.   Am I permitted to give my employees religious literature?

A.   As with spoken religious speech, employers can share their religious beliefs with their employees in print form such as pamphlets, books, and newsletters.[5] Employers must be careful, however, not to give employees the impression that they have to agree with the employer's religious beliefs in order to keep their job or get a promotion. For instance, in one case a Jewish employee was wrongfully terminated for complaining about the printing of Bible verses on his paychecks and the religious content of a company newsletter.[6] If an employer shares religious convictions with employees, and an employee disagrees or protests, no adverse action can be taken against the employee.

Furthermore, employers should be ready to accommodate any employee's objections to the religious speech contained in publications distributed to employees. Sufficient accommodation may be to provide the objecting employee with a publication that does not contain the religious content. In order to counter any impression given by publications that job security and advancement are contingent upon faith, it is also recommended that publications with religious material state that the employer does not discriminate on the basis of religion for purposes of continued employment, employee benefits, or promotion.

Q.   Can an employer hold regular prayer meetings or chaplain services for employees?

A.   Employers can hold regular devotional meetings for employees as long as attendance is not required.[7] Moreover, active participation of management in these meetings does not make them discriminatory.[8] To ensure that employees understand that devotional meetings are voluntary, notice of the meetings should state that they are not mandatory. Additionally, it is wise to hold these meetings before the workday begins, during breaks, or after work.

Q.   Can I require my employees to attend training based on biblical principles?

A.   Employers can use training programs that are based on the Bible. For instance, requiring an employee to attend a management seminar put on by the Institute of Basic Life Principles which used scriptural passages to support the lessons it sought to promote did not violate a Massachusetts civil rights law.[9] Employees cannot, however, be required to undergo religious training, participate in religious services, or engage in behavior that would violate their sincerely held religious beliefs.

Employee Religious Rights

Q.   Can I share the gospel with coworkers at work?

A.   If required by religious beliefs, an employee's religiously motivated expressions of faith are protected by Title VII. For instance, in conversations with other employees, you may refer to biblical passages on slothfulness and "work ethics."[10] Employees can engage in religious speech at work as long as there is no actual imposition on coworkers or disruption of the work routine.[11] Generally, no disruption of the work routine will occur if an employee's witnessing takes place during breaks, or other free time. If other employees are permitted to use electronic mail and screen savers for speech that is not related to work, an employee who has a sincerely held religious belief to communicate his faith with others should also be able to use these modes of communication.

To ensure that his religious speech is protected by Title VII, an employee should first of all be able to honestly say that his religious beliefs require him to share the gospel whenever possible with willing coworkers during breaks or other free time. The employee must then inform the employer of this religious belief (preferably in writing). At that point, the employer must attempt to accommodate this religious belief unless it will cause the employer "undue hardship."

Q.   Can I keep my Bible or other religious items at my desk?

A.   Yes. As with witnessing to coworkers, an employee can bring his Bible to work and keep it at his desk if he is required to do so by sincerely held religious beliefs. To ensure that this religious belief of having a Bible or other religious items at work is protected by Title VII, an employee should first of all be able to honestly say that his religious beliefs require him to bring these items to work. The employee must then inform the employer of this religious belief (preferably in writing). The employer is then required to attempt to accommodate this belief.

Q.   Is my employer permitted to restrict what I say when I am not at work?

A.   Employers generally cannot discriminate against employees because of religious speech expressed outside of the workplace.[12] The only possible exception is if speech activity engaged in outside the workplace directly affects the employee's ability to perform his job properly. For instance, even though not acting in their official capacity, judges have been prohibited from speaking out about issues on which they may have to rule.[13]

Q. What is Title VII and how does it protect employees?

A. The religious freedom of most employees is protected by a federal law called "Title VII."[14] In order to be protected by Title VII, an employee must show that: (1) he holds a sincere religious belief that conflicts with an employment requirement; (2) he has informed the employer about the conflict; and (3) he was discharged, disciplined, or subjected to discriminatory treatment for failing to comply with the conflicting employment requirement.[15]

1. Sincerely held religious belief.

The sincerity of religious belief is rarely at issue in Title VII cases. Although failure to act on a religious belief consistently may be considered evidence that the belief is not sincerely held,[16] the fact that the belief was only recently acquired does not render it an insincere one.[17] An employee is not held "to a standard of conduct which would have discounted his beliefs based on the slightest perceived flaw in the consistency of his religious practice."[18]

Religion under Title VII is broadly defined as including "all aspects of religious observance and practice, as well as belief."[19] The EEOC defines religious practices as including "moral or ethical beliefs as to what is right and wrong which are sincerely held with the strength of traditional religious views. . . . The fact that no religious group espouses such beliefs or the fact that the religious group to which the individual professes to belong may not accept such belief will not determine whether the belief is a religious belief of the employee."[20] In other words, the EEOC's test does not require that the employee's religious beliefs coincide with the tenets of his church: "Title VII protects more than the observance of Sabbath or practices specifically mandated by an employee's religion."[21] Religion under Title VII has been held to include the Black Muslim faith, the "old Catholic Religion," a "faith in humanity being," and atheism.[22] However, "religion" has not been so broadly defined as to include membership in the Ku Klux Klan, membership in the United Klans of America, or belief in the spiritual power of a certain cat food.[23]

2. Employee informed employer of religious belief.

Next the employee must show that the employer was aware of the belief. An employer has sufficient notice of an employee's religious belief if he has enough information about the employee's "religious needs to permit the employer to understand the existence of a conflict between employee's religious practices and the employer's job requirements."[24]

The best way to inform the employer is in writing. A simple letter to the employer stating: "I have a sincerely held religious belief to (or not to) _____. I am requesting that you, my employer, accommodate this sincerely held religious belief by allowing me to (or not requiring me to) _____." The employee should sign and date the letter, and keep a copy.

Notification in writing is not absolutely necessary, as long as the employer is aware of the beliefs.[25] A written notification, however, gives the employer a fair chance to attempt to accommodate your religious convictions by avoiding confusion or disputes over whether he actually had notice.[26]

This requirement must not be ignored. An employee's claim will be rejected if the employer does not understand the religious beliefs involved.[27]

3. Discriminatory treatment of employee.

If an employee can show he has a sincerely held religious belief and that the employer knew about it, Title VII prohibits the employer from discriminating against the employee because of the belief. "Discrimination" includes demotion, layoff, transfer, failure to promote, discharge, harassment, or intimidation, or the threat of these adverse employment actions.[28]

The employer is also required to reasonably accommodate the employee's religious beliefs unless such accommodation would result in undue hardship to the employer.[29] "Accommodation" means that employer neutrality is not enough.[30] In general, an employer is required to accommodate an employee's adherence to the principles of his religion unless such accommodation will actually interfere with the operations of the employer.

For more information on your rights as a Christian at work, contact:

The American Center for Law and Justice

P.O. Box 64429

Virginia Beach, VA 23467

(757) 226-2489

www.aclj.org

Notes

Chapter One

1. Dallas Willard, *The Spirit of the Disciplines* (San Francisco: HarperCollins, 1988), p. 214.
2. Tom Chappell, as quoted by Ben Cohen and Jerry Greenfield, *Ben & Jerry's Double Dip, Lead with Your Values and Make Money, Too* (New York: Simon & Schuster, 1997), pp. 238-239.
3. William C. Pollard, *The Soul of the Firm* (New York: HarperBusiness, 1996), pp. 18-19.

Chapter Two

1. Leona and Richard Bergstrom, *Amazing Grays, Unleashing the Power of Age in Your Congregation* (Bellingham, Wash.: Church Health, 2000), preface.
2. "One on One with Paul Klaassen," an interview in *Assisted Living Success*, April 2000.
3. Kerry Dolan, "Compassion Pays," *Forbes*, 24 February 1997.
4. Robert Banks, Kimberly Powell, Editors, *Faith in Leadership: How Leaders Live Out Their Faith in Their Work—and Why It Matters* (San Francisco: Jossey-Bass, 2000), p. 6.

Chapter Three

1. Joseph Jaworski as quoted by James E. Liebig, *Merchants of Vision: People Bringing New Purpose and Values to Business* (San Francisco: Berrett-Koehler, 1994), p. 13.
2. Michelle Conlin, "Religion in the Workplace," *BusinessWeek*, 1 November 1999, p. 54.

Chapter Four

1. Laura L. Nash, *Believers in Business: Resolving the Tensions between Christian Faith, Business Ethics, Competition and Our Definitions of Success* (Nashville: Nelson, 1994), p. 249.

Chapter Five

1. www.leadershipcatalyst.org/Who/Who1.htm.

2. Stephen R. Covey, *The Seven Habits of Highly Effective People* (New York: Simon & Schuster, 1989), p. 207.

3. Rolf Osterberg, as quoted by James E. Liebig, *Merchants of Vision: People Bringing New Purpose and Values to Business* (San Francisco: Berrett-Koehler, 1994), p. 25.

Chapter Six

1. *The River*, Garth Brooks, Victoria Shaw, BMG Songs, Inc., Major Bob Music Co., Inc., Mid-Summer Music Inc.

2. Michael F. Gerber, *The E-Myth Revisited: Why Most Small Businesses Don't Work and What to Do about It* (New York: HarperBusiness, 1995), p. 2.

3. Laura L. Nash, *Believers in Business: Resolving the Tensions between Christian Faith, Business Ethics, Competition and Our Definitions of Success* (Nashville: Nelson, 1994), p. 254.

4. William Diehl, as quoted by Robert Banks, Kimberly Powell, Editors, *Faith in Leadership: How Leaders Live Out Their Faith in Their Work—and Why It Matters* (San Francisco: Jossey-Bass, 2000), pp. 152-153.

Chapter Seven

1. Henri Nouwen, *In the Name of Jesus: Reflections on Christian Leadership* (New York: Crossroad, 1989), p. 67.

2. Charles Swindoll, *Hand Me Another Brick* (New York: Bantam Books, 1981), p. 22.

Chapter Eight

1. Dr. M. F. Bradford, as quoted by D. James Kennedy and Jerry Newcombe, *What If the Bible Had Never Been Written?* (Nashville: Nelson, 1998), p. 90.

2. Robert H. Bork, *Slouching Toward Gomorrah: Modern Liberalism and American Decline* (New York: HarperCollins, 1996), p. 277.

3. Philip Yancey, *What's So Amazing About Grace?* (Grand Rapids: Zondervan, 1997), p. 236.

4. John D. Beckett, *Loving Monday: Succeeding in Business Without Selling Your Soul* (Downers Grove, Ill.: InterVarsity, 1998), p. 96.

5. Marc Gunther, "God and Business," *Fortune*, 9 July 2001.

6. Beckett, p. 137.

Chapter Nine

1. Dennis Bakke, "Note from the Chairman," *The AES Corporation 2000 Annual Report*, p. 12.
2. Lawrence O. Richards, *Expository Dictionary of Bible Words*, s.v. "faithful."

Chapter Ten

1. Andrew Grove, *Only the Paranoid Survive* (New York: Doubleday, 1996), pp. 20-21.
2. "Silicon Values, An Interview with Paulina Borsook," *Christianity Today*, 6 August 2001, pp. 42-43.
3. Robert Howard, "Values Make the Company," *Harvard Business Review*, September-October 1990, pp. 138-39.
4. Scott Kirsner, "Nonprofit Motive," *Wired*, September 1999, p. 112.

Chapter Eleven

1. Merrill Oster and Mike Hamel, *The Entrepreneur's Creed* (Nashville: Broadman, 2001), pp. 51, 176-177.
2. James C. Collins and Jerry I. Porras, *Built to Last: Successful Habits of Visionary Companies* (New York: HarperBusiness, 1994), p. 222.

Chapter Twelve

1. Herman Cain, *Leadership Is Common Sense* (New York: Van Nostrand Reinhold, 1997), p. 164.
2. Kenneth Blanchard and Norman Vincent Peale, quoted by Kevin McCarthy in, *The On-Purpose Person: Making Your Life Make Sense* (Colorado Springs: Pinon Press, 1992), p. 79.

Chapter Thirteen

1. Richard Cimino and Don Lattin, *Shopping for Faith: American Religion in the New Millennium* (San Francisco: Jossey-Bass, 1998), p. 46.
2. Kent and Davidene Humphreys, *Show and Then Tell: Presenting the Gospel Through Daily Encounters* (Chicago: Moody, 2000), p. 47.

Chapter Fourteen

1. www.auntieannes.com/companyinfo/background.asp.

2. C. S. Lewis, *The Weight of Glory and Other Addresses* (Grand Rapids: Eerdmans, 1965), p. 2.

Chapter Fifteen

1. Robert H. Bork, *Slouching Toward Gomorrah: Modern Liberalism and American Decline* (New York: HarperCollins, 1996), pp. 273, 278.
2. Bork, p. 336.

Appendix

1. *Brown v. Polk County*, 61 F.3d 650 (8th Cir. 1995), *cert. den.*, 116 S. Ct. 1042 (1996).
2. *E.E.O.C. v. Townley Engineering & Mfg. Co.*, 859 F.2d 610, 621 (9th Cir. 1988).
3. *Meltebeke v. Bureau of Labor & Indus.*, 903 P.2d 351, 362-63 (Or. 1995) (evangelical Christian employer did not violate state law prohibiting employers from "making religious advances" by witnessing to his employee and inviting him to church).
4. *Chalmers*, 101 F.3d at 1021.
5. *Taylor v. National Group of Co's.*, 729 F. Supp. 575 (N.D. Ohio 1989) (employer's gift of a book endorsing secular humanism to new employees on their first day of work did not rise to the level of religious discrimination against a Christian employee).
6. *Brown Transport Corp. v. Human Relations Com'n.*, 578 A.2d 555 (Pa. Commw. Ct. 1990).
7. *Young v. Southwestern Sav. & Loan Assoc.*, 509 F.2d 140 (5th Cir. 1975).
8. *Brown v. Polk County*, 61 F.3d 650 (8th Cir. 1995), *cert. den.*, 116 S. Ct. 1042 (1996).
9. *Kolodziel v. Smith*, 588 N.F.2d 634 (Mass. 1992).
10. *Brown*, 61 F.3d at 652.
11. *Id.* at 657 (quoting *Burns v. Southern Pacific Transit Co.*, 589 F.2d 403, 407 (9th Cir. 1978), *cert. den.*, 439 U.S. 1072 (1979)). *See also* EEOC Dec. ¶ 6674 (1976), where an Orthodox Muslim was unlawfully fired for being "overzealous in his practices of his beliefs in his conversation with officers and inmates." The employer fired him because he "cannot be persuaded to tone down his religious practices on the job and continually gets wrapped up in conversations with the inmates." Because there was no evidence that the

employee's conduct had made him unable to perform his duties or hampered the efficient operation of the workplace, the employee prevailed in his claim.

12. CCH EEOC Dec. ¶ 6338.

13. *In re: Broadbelt*, 146 N.J. 501, 683 A.2d 543 (1996), *cert. den.*, 117 S. Ct. 1251 (1997); *See also Hollon v. Pierce*, 64 Cal. Rptr. 808 (Cal. Ct. App. 1967) (California human rights law was not violated by dismissal of school transportation supervisor who had, wholly apart from his employment, produced and distributed a religious tract that led school district to question supervisor's mental stability).

14. Title VII is codified at 42 U.S.C §§ 2000e *et seq.* It applies to virtually all employers with fifteen or more employees.

15. *Smith v. Pyro Mining*, 827 F.2d 1081,1085 (6th Cir. 1987), *cert den.*, 485 U.S. 989 (1988); *Heller v. EBB Auto Co.*, 8 F.3d 1433, 1438 (9th Cir. 1993); *Turpen v. Missouri-Kansas-Texas R. Co.*, 736 F.2d 1022, 1026 (5th Cir. 1984).

16. *Hansard V. Johns-Manville Products*, 5 EPD ¶ 8543 (E.D. Tex. 1973). *Compare Mississippi Employment Sec. Comm'n v. McGlothin*, 556 So. 2d 324 (Miss. 1990), *cert. den.*, 111 S. Ct. 211 (1990) (employee's belief was sincerely held even though she was not an active member of her religious group and wore her head wrap only occasionally).

17. *Cooper v. General Dynamics*, 378 F. Supp. 1258 (N.D. Tex. 1974), *rev'd on other grounds*, 533 F.2d 163 (5th Cir. 1976), *cert. den.*, 433 U.S. 908 (1977).

18. *E.E.O.C. v. University of Detroit*, 701 F. Supp. 1326, 1331 (E.D. Mich. 1988), *rev'd. on other grounds*, 904 F.2d 331 (6th Cir. 1990).

19. 42 U.S.C. 2000e(j). The courts and the EEOC have interpreted this provision very liberally. Donald T. Kramer; *Validity; Construction, and Application of Provisions of Title VII of the Civil Rights Act of 1964* (42 USCS §§ 2000e et seq.) and Implementing Regulations, Making Religious Discrimination in Employment Unlawful, 22 A.L.R. Fed. 580, 602 (1975).

20. Guidelines On Discrimination Because Of Religion, 29 CER § 1605.1.

21. *Heller*, 8 F.3d at 1438-39 (summarizing authorities); see also *Redmond v. GAF Corp.*, 574 F.2d 897 (7th Cir. 1978); 22 A.L.R. Fed. at 601-03.

22. EEOC Dec. No.71-2620 (1970); CCH EEOC Dec. ¶ 6823; EEOC Dec. No.71-779 (1970); CCH EEOC Dec. ¶ 6180; EEOC Dec. No.72-1301(1972); CCH EEOC Dec. ¶ 6338; *Young v. Southwestern Sav. & Loan Assoc.*, 509 F.2d 140 (5th Cir. 1975).

23. EEOC Dec. No.79-06 (1978), CCH EEOC Dec. ¶ 6737; *Bellamy v. Mason's*

Stores, 368 F. Supp. 1025 (E.D. Va. 1973), *aff'd.*, 508 F.2d 504 (4th Cir. 1974); *Brown V. Pena*, 441 F. Supp. 1382 (S.D. Fla. 1977), *aff'd*, 589 F.2d 1113 (5th Cir. 1982).

24. *Heller*, 8 F.3d at 1439.

25. *Brown v. Polk County*, 61 F.3d 650, 654-55 (8th Cir. 1995), *cert. den.*, 116 S Ct. 1042 (1996).

26. *See Chalmers v. Tulon Co.*, 101 F.3d 1012 (4th Cir. 1996).

27. *Chrysler Corp. v. Mann*, 561 F.2d 1282, 1285-86 (8th Cir. 1977), *cert. den.*, 434 U.S. 1039 (1978).

28. Gregory S. Samo, *Harassment or Termination of Employee Due to Religious Beliefs or Practices*, 35 P.O.F.2d 209, 222 (1983) (hereinafter "Harassment"); *EEOC v. Townley Eng'g and Mfg.*, 859 F.2d 610, 614 n.5 (4th Cir 1988), *cert. den.*, 489 U.S. 1077 (1989).

29. *Trans World Airlines v. Hardison*, 432 U.S. 63, 73-74 (1977); *EEOC v. READS, Inc.*, 759 F. Supp. 1150, 1155 (E.D. Pa. 1991); 29 C.F.R. § 1605.2(c).

30. *Riley v. Bendix Corp.*, 464 F.2d 1113, 1115 (5th Cir. 1972); *Reid v. Memphis Publishing Co.*, 468 F.2d 346, 350-51 (6th Cir. 1972) (the fact that a particular policy is applied uniformly to all employees does not lessen the discriminatory effect upon a particular employee's religious beliefs).

Meet the Contributors

Chapter One   Service Call

Bill Pollard is the chairman of the executive committee of the board of The ServiceMaster Company. He joined the company in 1977 and has served twice as its CEO. He is a graduate of Wheaton College and earned his J.D. from Northwestern University School of Law. He is also a director or trustee of a number of educational, religious, and nonprofit organizations, including Wheaton College and The Drucker Foundation. He is chairman of the executive committee of the Billy Graham Evangelistic Association.

Mr. Pollard is the author of the bestselling book *The Soul of the Firm*, and has contributed to numerous books and magazines. He is actively involved in teaching and speaking on subjects relating to management, ethics, and integrating faith and work. A native of Chicago, Bill and his wife, Judy, have been married for more than forty years. They have four adult children and twelve grandchildren.

Chapter Two   The Business of True Religion

Paul and Teresa (Terry) Klaassen are founders of Sunrise Living, Inc., one of America's largest assisted living providers. They started Sunrise in 1981 because of the lack of long-term care options for their own loved ones. Today, with over two hundred communities in twenty-six states, Canada, and the U.K., Sunrise serves almost fifteen thousand residents and their families.

Paul is also the chairman of The Trinity Forum, a nonprofit organization devoted to the renewal of American society through the transformation of leaders. Terry has received numerous awards, including the 1993

Greater Washington, D.C. Entrepreneur of the Year Award. She is a member of The Committee of 200, a leadership group of select corporate women in the U.S., and a member of the International Women's Forum. The Klaassens have been married over twenty-three years and have three children.

Chapter Three   Built to Last

David Weekley grew up in a godly home in Houston and became a Christian at a Young Life camp in Colorado. He was graduated from Trinity University in San Antonio with degrees in economics and geology. While waiting to attend the M.B.A. program at Harvard, he started his own homebuilding company in 1976. Ten years later, he was the National Association of Homebuilders' Builder of the Year. In 2000, and again in 2001, *Fortune* ranked his company as one of the 100 Best Companies to Work For.

David has served on the vestry at Palmer Memorial Church. He is the past president of the Houston Chapter of the Young Presidents Organization and the Greater Houston Builder's Association. He serves on the steering committee of Metro Houston Young Life and on the board of trustees for Kinkaid School. David and his wife Bonnie have been married since 1976 and have three children.

Chapter Four   24/7

Ken Eldred is the founder of Inmac, the first company to market computer products via catalog. He was also involved in the founding or developing of a number of companies, including ClickAction, Office Depot, and Norm Thompson Outfitters, Inc. In 1988 the Institute of American Entrepreneurs named him Retail Entrepreneur of the Year for the San Francisco Bay Area.

In 1996, Ken left Inmac and helped start Ariba Technologies, Inc., an Internet-B2B platform based on a concept he developed. He is also the chairman of Parakletos@Ventures. For over twenty years, he has been an advisor to Crosspoint Venture Partners. He and his wife, Roberta, started Living Stones Foundation, a public support organization to encourage Christian work around the world. The Eldreds live in Silicon Valley and have three grown sons.

Chapter Five   Custom Fit

Dale Gifford is the chief executive of Hewitt Associates, LLC, a billion-dollar business. The product of a small Wisconsin town, he joined the firm in 1972 after graduating with honors from the University of Wisconsin. Hewitt had about one hundred and forty associates at the time. Today it has nearly thirteen thousand working in thirty-seven countries.

Mr. Gifford assisted in the management of the firm's actuarial practice, led their flexible compensation practice, managed the Southwest and Midwest regions, and directed international operations prior to becoming chief executive in 1992. He is a fellow of the Society of Actuaries and vice chairperson of EBRI (Employee Benefit Research Institute). He also serves on the board of Leadership Catalyst Inc. Dale and Becky Gifford have three children and one grandchild.

Chapter Six   Owner's Privilege

Ray Berryman is chairman of the board and CEO of Berryman & Henigar Enterprises, a firm he started in 1975. Today it has evolved into two companies with more than nine hundred employees and annual revenues in excess of $40 million. Ray has a B.S. in engineering and has done postgraduate studies in civil engineering.

Mr. Berryman serves on the boards of several Christian organizations, including: the executive committee of History's Handful, a ministry of Campus Crusade for Christ International; Priority Associates, a ministry committed to reaching businesspeople and leaders in the marketplace; Food for the Hungry, a ministry committed to relief and strategic development in needy areas of the world; and Capitol Ministries, which tends to the spiritual needs of state legislators in various states. He and his wife Mary have six children and ten grandchildren.

Chapter Seven   Celebrating Diversity

Donna Auguste earned her undergraduate degree from the University of California, Berkeley, in computer science and electrical engineering in 1980, and then entered the Carnegie-Mellon Institute's graduate program in computer science. After college she held important positions at IntelliCorp, Apple Computer, and US West before cofounding her own software company in 1996.

Donna is also the founder of the Leave a Little Room Foundation, which exists to share the gifts of gospel music, education, food, clothing, housing, technology, and other resources. Music has always been important to Donna. She has been a church musician since 1984 and is currently the bass player for the gospel choirs of Cure d'Ars Catholic Church in Denver, where she also codirects the children's choir.

Chapter Eight   Rights and Responsibilities

John Beckett is a native of Elyria, Ohio. He was graduated from M.I.T. in 1960 with a B.S. in economics and mechanical engineering. When his father died unexpectedly in 1963, John became president of the R. W. Beckett Corporation. He now serves as its chairman and CEO.

John is the author of the bestselling *Loving Monday: Succeeding in Business Without Selling Your Soul.* He helped found Intercessors For America in 1973 and continues as its chairman. He is a founding board member of the International Leadership University and serves on the boards of Henry Blackaby Ministries and Concerts of Prayer International. In 1999 the Christian Broadcasting Network named John the "Christian Businessman of the Year." He and Wendy have been married over forty years and have six children and seven grandchildren.

Chapter Nine   Business As Stewardship

Dennis Bakke is cofounder, president, and CEO of The AES Corporation. Formed in 1981 to generate and sell electricity, AES has grown into a global power company with a presence in fifteen countries. Prior to starting AES, Dennis served as the executive assistant to the administrator of the Federal Energy Administration and later became the deputy manager for energy conservation programs. He left FEA to attend the National War College, graduating with distinction in 1977.

Mr. Bakke currently serves as director of Young Life of Washington, D.C., cofounder and president of the Mustard Seed Foundation, board member of the Council for Excellence in Government, and board member of Electric Power Supply Association. He is married to the former Eileen Harvey. They have five children.

Chapter Ten   High (Tech) Calling

Greg Newman was the cofounder of C2B Technologies, a company that provided web-based shopping engines to Internet portals. Prior to his success with C2B, which was sold in 1998, Greg was the director of marketing for e-commerce and Internet technologies at Oracle. He was also one of the original members of the Macromedia marketing team, and while at Apple Computers, he served as senior product manager for QuickTime, the industry standard in cross-platform multimedia software.

Today, Greg is a senior partner with Integrity Partners, a venture capital firm focused on investments in high-tech start-ups. He also devotes his time and resources to EquipNet, a ministry he started to work with indigenous Christian leaders around the world. Greg and Jeanine Newman have been married since 1984 and have four children.

Chapter Eleven   Family Litehouse

Doug Hawkins is a native of Sandpoint, Idaho. He was graduated from the University of Idaho in 1966 with a degree in physical education, and after coaching and teaching for three years, he returned to the family restaurant business. Edward Hawkins Jr. followed in his older brother's footsteps, getting his elementary education degree in 1974 and teaching until 1977, when he joined Litehouse Foods full-time. Today, Doug heads up sales and marketing, while Edward Jr. directs operations and finance.

The Hawkins brothers are active in their community, having served on the city council and the Bonner County Economic Development Committee. In their respective local churches they have served in such roles as Sunday school teacher, youth leader, deacon, and building committee member. Doug is married and has six children and four grandchildren. Edward Jr. is married and has four children.

Chapter Twelve   Living On-Target

Albert Black Jr. was born and raised in the Frazier Courts housing projects in South Dallas. He was graduated from the University of Texas and earned his M.B.A. from Southern Methodist University in 1982. That same year he and his wife, Gwyneith Navon Black, founded what is now On-Target Supplies & Logistics, a business that serves industrial clients in several states.

Mr. Black has served as chairman of the Greater Dallas Chamber of Commerce and is on the advisory board of TXU-Dallas and the Chase Bank, Dallas, board of directors. He has received numerous awards, including the 30th Congressional District Award for Outstanding Achievement in Business, the Quest for Success Award from the Dallas Black Chamber of Commerce, and the Ernst & Young Southwest Region Entrepreneur of the Year Award. Albert and Gwyneith have three children.

Chapter Thirteen   Doctor's Advice

Dr. David Parsons was a fighter pilot and winner of the Top Gun award in three fighter aircraft. He flew more than four hundred and fifty combat sorties during the Vietnam War. While in the Air Force he also decided to become a surgeon. He went on to graduate with honors from the University of Texas and completed both a pediatric residency in San Antonio and Otolaryngology/Head and Neck Surgery residency at the University of Colorado.

Colonel Parsons retired from the Air Force in 1993. In 1998 he entered private practice in Greenville, South Carolina, where he's also a clinical professor at the University of South Carolina. He has designed more than forty surgical instruments and published over one hundred and twenty-five medical articles. He has also been named among the top 1,000 doctors in America. David is active in medical missionary work. He and his wife, Barbara (Begee), have three children and four grandchildren.

Chapter Fourteen   Little Rewards, Big Rewards

Anne Beiler grew up Amish-Mennonite in Lancaster County, Pennsylvania. At the age of twelve she began her business career by baking cakes and pies to sell at local farmers' markets. In 1987 she took a job managing a concession stand in a farmers' market to support her husband's vision of providing free counseling services. In 1988 the Beilers bought their own stand and perfected their pretzel recipe.

The pretzels were so good that Anne has gone from bagging pretzel mix in her garage to overseeing a corporate staff of more than one hundred and supporting a franchise system with over seven hundred locations worldwide. In 1992, Jonas and Anne Beiler opened the Family Resource and Counseling Center. Six years later they created the Angela Foundation, a nonprofit organization that serves as the giving arm for Auntie Anne's. The Beilers have two children and two grandchildren.

Chapter Fifteen   Crisis Management

Merrill Oster is an international business journalist, publishing entrepreneur, and author of seven books. He has founded or built several businesses and lectures widely on world business issues. He was involved with the Young Presidents Organization (YPO) for over ten years and is a past recipient of the Iowa Entrepreneur of the Year Award, as well as one of thirteen recipients of the Entrepreneur of the Century Award for the Cedar Valley area.

In 1996, Merrill became a founder of Pinnacle Forum, a group seeking to positively influence the culture of America. The Forum creates venues where the cultural gatekeepers of the nation can explore the connection between issues of faith and society. Merrill and his wife, Carol, have two children and six grandchildren.

Meet the Authors

CHRISTOPHER A. CRANE won the 1999 USA Today / Ernst and Young Entrepreneur of the Year Award in San Diego. In 1992, he bought COMPS InfoSystems, Inc., and grew it into the largest commercial real estate sales information company in the US. He did four rounds of venture financing, took it public, and, in 2000, sold the company.

Chris studied art and economics at the University of Vienna and earned his B.S. in finance *summa cum laude* from Boston College and his M.B.A. from Harvard Business School in 1976. He and his wife, the former Jane Leonard, have been married for nineteen years and have one son, Andrew. They live in La Jolla, California.

MIKE HAMEL is a former pastor who served churches in Colorado, Oregon, and Illinois for more than fifteen years. He has interviewed scores of business leaders for his various books. He is the author or coauthor of several works. His nonfiction titles include *The Women's Ministry Handbook* and *The Entrepreneur's Creed*. His articles have appeared in *Life@Work*, *First Priority*, and *Focus on the Family* magazines.

Mike and his wife, Susan, have been married over twenty-eight years. They live in Colorado Springs, Colorado, and have four grown children.

CHANGE YOUR BUSINESS, CAREER, AND LIFE!

The On-Purpose Business

Do you love your work? Do your job and business truly make a difference? *The On-Purpose Business* helps you address these and other critical questions.
(Kevin W. McCarthy)

Entrepreneurs of Life

Through the writings of men and women who fought slavery, reinvented healthcare, or composed great music, you'll find models to follow as you discover and answer your life's calling.
(Os Guinness)

Connecting

No one is capable of living life without help. Learn how mentoring relationships can put you years ahead of where you'd be on your own.
(Paul D. Stanley & J. Robert Clinton)

To get your copies, visit your local bookstore, call 1-800-366-7788, or log on to www.navpress.com. Ask for a FREE catalog of NavPress products. Offer #BPA.

NAVPRESS
BRINGING TRUTH TO LIFE
www.navpress.com